HOPE

A PLAY BY
DECLAN TAN

MONTAG

First Montag Press E-Book and Paperback Original Edition July 2017

Montag Press
ISBN: 978-1-940233-43-7
Front cover art © Akte One (www.akteone.de) and Street Art Berlin (www.streetartbln.com)
Cover photo © Michael A. Mason & Sarah Schwarz
Interior book design and jacket © 2017 Niall Gray
Editor & Managing Director – Charlie Franco

A Montag Press Book
www.montagpress.com
Montag Press
1066 47th Ave. Unit #9
Oakland CA 94601 USA

Montag Press, the burning book with the hatchet cover, the skewed word mark and the portrayal of the long-suffering fireman mascot are trademarks of Montag Press.

Printed & Digitally Originated in the United States of America
10 9 8 7 6 5 4 3 2 1

"Smart and funny with a wicked sense of the absurd, Declan Tan's *HOPE* is not satisfied with mere wordplay, and digs deeply into the lives of its characters, always asking what good really is hope (if it's any good at all)."

— David L. Williams, playwright, *The Winners* and *Ampersand*

For Vera,
always

Setting

Charity shop, unknown time of day.

Characters

HAVELOCK, *early sixties, regular build, gaunt face*
ELLIS, *late-sixties, overweight, squat, fake Irish accent*
RICHEY, *late-teens, baby face, Adidas tracksuit*
FRANCIS, *early thirties, smartly dressed, goatee, Australian*
NADIA, *mid-thirties, business dress, large, tight bun of hair*
BLUE CARDIGAN GIRL, *late-twenties/early thirties, bohemian, nervous, cute*
MIDDLE-AGED MAN, *scruffy, torn shirt, long coat, boils on face*
MOTHER, *with pram*
CHILD, *red raincoat*
EDIE, *sixties, white hair, plump*
SOPHIA, *late-fifties, jeans and jacket*
TV NEWS READER, *unseen*
OLIVER SCHREINER, *Ladbrokes manager, unseen*
CUSTOMER/MAN, *construction worker*

Synopsis

Two ageing homeless men, the bitter Ellis and the recently be-reaved Havelock (Hal), thrust together by fate, share the shop floor of a charity shop, H.O.P.E., their last refuge from troubled pasts.

In light of ailing sales (nobody wants dated, sticky DVDs any-more), the property is put up for sale. A young couple from the City sweep in to purchase, looking to escape the rat race and realise their dreams of opening a coffee shop/yoga school/bookshop called The Hippo Campus. Even as the sale looks set to go through, Hal becomes increasingly convinced he can rescue the shop, to save himself, his newfound home, his dignity – and Ellis (but only if he has to) – while Ellis, still seething from Hal's invasion, does all he can to sabotage their efforts. Throw into the mix a sketchy young volunteer, Richey, and an overly curious, be-cardiganned customer, and there's no telling what might finally become of H.O.P.E. – or if Hal and Ellis can hold out that long...

Running Time: approx. 90-95 mins

"The place where optimism most flourishes is the lunatic asylum."

- Havelock Ellis

Act I
Scene One

Charity shop. Shutters down. Glass door and window display centre stage left, front of shutters. Directly over the store's front shutters is the mechanism to raise them. Clock above door rear, right, clock hands at 12. Soft individual spotlights on two elderly men: one sleeping soundly, the other stirring, about to wake.

ELLIS, *in his late-sixties, portly set, stubby but agile-seeming, sleeps. A thick, drawn-back shock of white hair rises from his head and every possible orifice: ears, nose, even knuckle, with a tartan blanket (sales tag attached) pulled up to his chin. He sports a pair of ornately threaded pointy black boots with worn heels; they're otherwise squeaky clean poking out from under his blanket, as if recently polished up for display. He's cosily tucked in – the kind of tucked in that somebody else has to do for you. A lamp nearby dimly shines on* **ELLIS** *lightly snoring.*

VOICE (*off, booming, ominous*): Hope and Despair, the torturers, slept.

HAVELOCK *wakes with a start. He is younger, thinner and slightly taller. He wears shoes with fresh tread, which he uses to loom over* **ELLIS** *whenever he can.* **HAVELOCK** *fashions a loose fitting, itchy-looking dark green and mustard tweed suit straight off the rack, presumably not paid for – the price tag hangs from the sleeve. He also wears a pork pie hat – to add height to his looming. Price tag attached.*

HAVELOCK *sits in a plush armchair squeezing his knee caps, gripping the bones, awake by now and wringing every vein in his body to remain conscious. He nervously removes and replaces his hat now and then, twitching his head intermittently from side to side, flashing his eyes toward the closed shutters.*

HAVELOCK *and* **ELLIS** *are each in unlikely members' armchairs of matching Chesterfield red leather with dark rosewood feet as polished as their shoes. Both chairs still have their price tags. Everything does.*

The shop's interior is wide. A sign with the letters H-O-P-E sits askew over the shop's till, centre rear. In front of the till is a cabinet of watches and trinkets. The lights slowly come up to reveal more of the shop. Gold-framed "Head on a Green Sofa" by Lucian Freud, back wall, next to a torn film poster for Fassbinder's Despair. *A painting of a half-nude 19th century lady looking furtively over her bare shoulder hangs crooked on the wall, back left.*

The space is gutted of almost all for-sale items. The shop floor stretches out to the back of stage where the doorway, back right, next to the painting, leads down some steps. There are random stacks of unwanted books leaning along the skirting boards half fallen over. Near-empty clothing rails, sparsely filled cabinets of decorative plates and various miscellany run along the right wall. The bookshelves have almost all been emptied; one or two paperbacks have been absentmindedly left here and there as if someone had picked them up then tossed them aside. Two chest-height standalone bookcases divide the room into sections, on them are various items including: a large dictionary, a metronome, used mugs, plates, toenail clippers, used cutlery and porcelain ornaments. The cutlery has been thrown haphazardly into a used and open picnic set (all price-tagged). Tipped-over glasses are in shelves and on floors, suggestions of alcohol consumption, take-away boxes, a small ticking alarm clock, an empty stained-glass fruit bowl, and a torn multipack of Monster Munch, with emptied packets strewn about. There are more items by the feet of ELLIS *and* HAVELOCK, *and a blanket each.*

HAVELOCK (*hacking cough*): She'll ... (*clears throat*) she'll not be along ... not for a while yet. Not to worry. No trouble. (*pause*) Nae bother, he'd say.

ELLIS *snores.*

HAVELOCK: Aye.

HAVELOCK *shifts and squeaks in his seat. He slowly gets up and shuffles around the room amongst the mess. He touches a shelf, runs his finger along it checking for dust before rubbing it between his fingers. (long pause) He puts the finger on his tongue and winces, then dabs it some more.*

HAVELOCK: Can't be time yet, no. (*pause*) Hm. (*pause*) Bringing the news. Harbinger of. (*pause*) I'll just ... y'know. Explain to her. No. Pay it no mind, he'd say. (*sucks his finger, pause*) Pay no mind.

HAVELOCK *twitches as if sensing something in the room, standing behind* ELLIS's *armchair.* HAVELOCK *moves his head to see but is not alarmed. His eyes follow something as it slowly crosses the room and descends the stairs at rear.*

HAVELOCK: Night then. (*pause*) Bye – *forever*, he'd say. (*pause*) No. Wouldn't say that at all would he. (*pause*) Hasn't the wit. The human ... the humour.

HAVELOCK *slumps back down in his armchair. Sighs.*

ELLIS (*snores*): Mghm ...

HAVELOCK: It's only ... (*looking to clock*) 12? Only 12. (*relieved*) We're grand. She won't be 'long 'til the next day. Long time yet. Hours. Half a day even. Things hoped for. (*pause*) Plenty to do first, o'course. But plenty ... Lots of it. *This* is all that matters.

ELLIS (*stirs momentarily, continues snoring*): Mghmhm ...

HAVELOCK: Bleedin' *horde* of time is what we've got on our hands here. (*looking around*) I mean, there might be a bit of mess, sure. Not, in precise terms, at least, not in some schools of thought, a *substantial* amount of merchandise to shift. You wouldn't be wrong there. There's no mistaking that. No mistaking it, he'd say. I mean. Look at it. (*turning to* ELLIS, *sniffs, distracted*) Smells like a snooker table in here, or doesn't it? (*pause*) S'all musty, like. Smells of – oul' crusty curtains. And cigarettes. Smells of oul' curtains and snooker and cigarettes. Or's that me? (*smells himself*) Curtains. (*looking at* **ELLIS**) And this one. The pink ball. The fat on him. Fat of face and a ... mashed-up sausage roll for the rest. All that sugar all'a time. All that sugar in the brew. And on the, on the cornflakes. On the sangwidges. Tubby shite.

HAVELOCK *moves to get up again but thinks better of it.*

HAVELOCK (*suddenly*): I said, Oi! (*raising his voice*) Oi, chubber! (*quietly*) I *said*: she'll not be here for a while yet – better get some rest! (*pause*) Snoring away. Be here by 9, she said.

As he says 9, **HAVELOCK** *turns his head toward the wall again. Shakes his head awake to see better, not believing what it says: that it's still exactly 12.*

HAVELOCK: Wakey wakey for opening-up time ...

The shutters are down, we don't know whether it's day or night. **HAVE-LOCK** *looks down at his wrist, drawing back the sleeve – he has no watch. He looks across at* **HAVELOCK**, *suddenly, accusingly.*

HAVELOCK: HEY!

ELLIS *still doesn't shift – remains snoring, tucked up tight.*

HAVELOCK: AY! (*hysterical for a moment, then suddenly calm, scheming*) Me feckin' watch! He's got me feckin' watch the fat bogue! (**HAVELOCK** *jabs down at his wrist, thrusting it out toward* **ELLIS**) Hey, you thieving pimp ya!

Long pause.

ELLIS (*sighs, eyes still closed*): That there's *my* watch. (*pause*) Always has been. (*pause, deliberately*) You seen that one 'side the cabinet, boyo – you'rn? Feast your eyes on that buffet [*pronounced:* 'buff-ett'] of delights. (*pause*) Tick on, son. Two quid. (*pause*) Want it back? (*clears throat with no small effort*) Two quid.

HAVELOCK (*remembering*): Oh, ah, yes. Quite right.

ELLIS: Want it back – cost ya' two quid. Like I said. Yep. Forgot that didn't you. Forgot that again. (*licks his lips*) *Slipped* your *mind*. (*pause, licks lips*) Having a kip now, aye. (*pause*) Keep it shtum now yeah. Fellas kippin' 'ere.

HAVELOCK (*quietly*): You go on back to sleep. Sophia'll not be along for a good while yet. You go on ahead, get your nut down.

ELLIS (*eyes still shut*): Why don't you go an' get your nut down an' all?

HAVELOCK: No point sleeping now, not me – no good for the, for the mind. The body. Awake now and awake it'll stay.

ELLIS: Days it's been. Days on end. It's no good for ye.

HAVELOCK: You're welcome to kip, El. It'll do you good. Of course. (*longer pause*) What time are we, El?

ELLIS'*s eyes open at last, exasperated. Still licking his lips, looking around agitated with thirst or hunger.*

ELLIS: Git' me me sammich I'll tell ya. Any time you like I'll tell ya.

HAVELOCK (*distracted, still twitching and looking at clock*): The sangwidge? What's that then.

ELLIS: It was ... em – up there, it was. And a cuppa. Git me me sammich, next to that dinosaur book so it is ... (*leaning head forward slightly*) And a cuppa. (*alarmed*) Sure where's it gone – where've you moved it to?

HAVELOCK (*turning back slowly*): I've … not the foggiest what you're on … it's … (*pause*) The dinosaur book? Up there, isn't it. Can see the Triceratopses.

ELLIS: Wha', it's what? All your messin' sure an' now you've gone and lost it, me feckin' mustard and ham sammich!

HAVELOCK: No, it's there somewhere. You bring it downstairs the last time? Didn't you? Must have – you tell us the time I'll more'n happily go below 'n' fetch it. You tell me where it is. I'd be happy to, for a pal. Just say the word.

ELLIS *looks suspiciously upon* HAVELOCK. *With great ceremony,* ELLIS *pulls out an arm from the taut blanket and looks down at his left wrist, reading the time to himself slowly from his wristwatch (also with a tiny but visible price tag). It takes him a good while longer than it should, staring at it, and he does it silently, blinking, looking up at* HAVELOCK, *then back to the watch.* ELLIS *lifts his head as if finally he has taken a reading.* ELLIS *goes to open his mouth.*

HAVELOCK (*leaning in*): Mm yes? (*pause*) Well? Then what is it? What is it, what are we?

ELLIS *doesn't speak.*

HAVELOCK: Go ahead … no holding back now. What time are we? Let it rip, lad.

Long pause.

ELLIS *tilts his head to read the time again. He stares down, blinking slowly.*

HAVELOCK: Yes?

ELLIS: Ahem.

HAVELOCK: Come on now – even a blasted child reads time. It isn't difficult! You just look and you *know*, you know? You just look at it 'n' it reads itself – even an *idiot* child can muster that *much*.

Long pause.

Look, it doesn't take that long! (*almost weeping*) It just doesn't take *anyone* that long!

ELLIS (*raising head slowly*): An idiot child, is it? Get us me sammich first – sure isn't it even the rats and the vermin of this earth what can find sammiches and the like in no time at all. A snap of the fingers for the bolloxed rats even. The manky shite ones. Are you worse than a manky shite bolloxed rat, Hal? Eh? Is that the news you're deliverin' me on this morn? (*looks away, suddenly, having given it away*)

HAVELOCK: Don't talk news.

ELLIS: And it won't be the only shite bit of news we'll be having. Pff. *An idiot child.* (*looking back*) Would ya' listen to'm.

As **ELLIS** *speaks, he squeaks the leather armchair, leaning his head forward. He stares blinking at* **HAVELOCK**'s *feet. Pause.*

HAVELOCK (*realising, standing*): Morn? Morning then, is it? What? Already? But we haven't scrubbed up!

ELLIS: Whu'fuh! (*agitated*) Hup! Hup! What's that be your hoof there? (*screeching*) Hal!

HAVELOCK: What. (*looking down, picking up his feet absentmindedly as if for a passing hoover*) Where. (*he takes up a nearby book, something like a children's dinosaur encyclopaedia and flips it open, sits*) Hold your flapping and give us the hour, would ya – we're going extinct here.

ELLIS: Me sammich! (*struggling to get out of his seat, somehow stuck, panicked*)

HAVELOCK: What *are* you gassing on about. (*turns away to clock, flicking through the pages blindly*) Look the time's *stopped*, El – it must have. Precisely on 12 to be exact. Which is a bit ... eerie. If I'm honest. So you've gotta' tell me. The time it is now and not the half hour ago when you were asked. (*turning back, gesturing toward the shutters*)

ELLIS *is slowly trying to get up but is so tightly tucked in at the legs he can't manage it. He kicks them out a little in an attempt to break free. As* **ELLIS** *struggles,* **HAVELOCK** *continues blithely.*

ELLIS: This is ridiculous! Who in feckin' dusty crusted fecks 'as tucked me in this tight?

HAVELOCK: A half hour ago I ask him the time, a half hour ago when he damn well wouldn't speak! When otherwise it's non-stop blather from him. *Now* he clams up. (*pause*) Well we've to open up the shop, haven't we – if it's opening-up time. Surely, isn't that why they call it opening-up time and isn't that what shops do. You see that, yes?

ELLIS *is exhausted with struggling, takes a break.*

You do understand that fundamental. No use in the rising, the untucking of blankets, all that pressing of buttons, lifting and airing the arms, the shutters, windows, those too, and letting all that – *that* in – when we have to *clean up*, mop the floors – that'd be enough in itself, but then the plates of course for suppin' the mornin's milk – and if it's not *opening-up* time, then for why? (*twitchy*) You see that, yes. Surely?

ELLIS (*frantic*): See?

HAVELOCK: He sees, at last.

ELLIS: Seen is what I bloody well have, ya' feck! (**ELLIS** *finally manages to break free of his blanket and jumps to his feet with a bang of his boots. In the spotlight, under the blanket we see he is wearing a garish, matching Adidas tracksuit with hoody, far too tight for his large gut, the tracksuit bottoms tucked into the boots – all with price tags*) Scoffed it! (*looking down at his clothes*) What tae feck's gone on here?!

ELLIS *storms forward to* **HAVELOCK** *in his chair, who throws his hands up to protect his face as* **ELLIS**, *instead of striking him, hesitates, swoops down and grabs up the empty box. He stares seething into the empty packaging. He goes over to the far wall and switches on the light. We see the true state of the shop until now concealed.*

ELLIS: Begob the pig's scoffed it! (*voice shrill and rising*) Gone and bleeding well scoffed the lot! Not a crumb left in the feck!

HAVELOCK (*seeing the evidence thrust in his face, but not really comprehending*): Alright, alright I'll owe you! I'll git' you another. How much hey?

ELLIS *turns around to conceal the reduced stickers and slowly looks over the box. The final price is too small to read, but it's about 23p.*

ELLIS: Four-fifty these are worth! And you ain't got nae feckin' money anyhow!

ELLIS *throws the box at* HAVELOCK*'s face, looks around for something to beat him with. During this* ELLIS *shouts and rants.* ELLIS *picks up a spoon and throws it downward at* HAVELOCK*'s head. It's plastic. Then a paperback (e.g.* The Dice Man, Game of Thrones, *or some other heavy, frequently found charity shop paperback).* HAVELOCK *blocks his face.* ELLIS *throws the picnic set with a clatter. In the rush to grab more,* ELLIS *knocks the metronome, setting it off. Quick tempo. He runs out of nearby things to launch at* HAVELOCK. *He searches about.*

ELLIS (*calming for a moment then, seeing the package, bites his lip again in anger*): Give me that feckin' cap, you!

HAVELOCK, *cowering, slams his hands down on his head, then pulling down the brim.* ELLIS *whips it away with one flick of the wrist.* HAVELOCK *is weaker than he looks.*

ELLIS (*viciously*): Mark my words and mark them well, Havelock – you greedy, inconsiderate pighole. You'll never hear your precious time now so you won't. (ELLIS *hocks up phlegm, spits down into the hat, and slowly and menacingly places it back on* HAVELOCK*'s head*) Mark my words boyo. (*pause, quietly, turning*) First he takes the bed. Then the ... (*gesturing around*) the *this*. (*pause*) And then finally – me feckin' sammiches. The last straw so it is.

Beat.

HAVELOCK (*removing the hat and placing it down at his feet, calmly*): You're always like this when you've not eaten. (*pause*) Hangry's what they're calling it now.

ELLIS: And whose bloody fault is *that*? (ELLIS *walks calmly over to the clock, takes it off its hook and frisbees it at the shop window.* HAVELOCK *turns to the wall.*) Eating up the feckin' supplies, ya' greedy feckin' pig bung!

HAVELOCK: Just calm down would you. (*petulantly*) How could you possibly ... And anyway, it was *12*! I don't need *that* thing.

ELLIS: Oh. Aye (*looks to clock, calms down*) 12? (*pointing to the clock on the floor*) Believe *that* do you? Well happy New Year then! ... Look. It's obviously fecked! You said so yoursel'. (*Now stamping on it*) Believe anything you're fecking well told, you! (*still stamping*) Even be stamped-on clocks! (*pause, pointing down, satisfied*) ... So what time are we *now* then?

HAVELOCK (*tries to read it from his seat, but can't*): Happy New Year ... (*picks up a nearby Guinness Book of Records*) 19 ... 96?

ELLIS: Doesn't even know what year.

HAVELOCK: 1996 and it's ... (*reading the clock*) a quarter and 2 to 6?

ELLIS: Even an *idiot* child, wasn't it? Well done. Oh. And it's not *even* New Year's yet is it, feckin' eej.

HAVELOCK (*grinning, reading the clock, long pause*): Twelvty past twen?

ELLIS: He keeps on.

HAVELOCK: You're the stamped-on clock, you – you rotten codging fish. It's 12. It doesn't make the blindest bit of difference your talkin' now. (*pause, folding his arms*) It'll *always* be 12 to me.

ELLIS: You're not feckin' far off there, pal. It *will* always be ... *stopped* time to you. (*pause*) Because I don't know what – you're all biscuits in the head, man. Like a ... a ... a kicked-about pack'f biscuits, you – Digestives – 'at's you, aye – the dust that be's in the bottom. Af'er all the whole proper biscuits've gone.

ELLIS *grabs the metronome, grabbing it roughly with a fist – before slamming it on the floor, smashing it to pieces.*

HAVELOCK (*quietly, to the silenced metronome rhythm*): It was 12. 12. 12. 12. (*thinking*) That means we've still ... (*counting*) 9 whole entire hours!

ELLIS (*playing along, exhausted into almost seeing the funny side*): Well. Prove it.

HAVELOCK: Pff. I don't have to. Just *know* it was. Is. 12. Can just tell.

ELLIS: ... Can just tell, can you? The time? Well good for you! Lord Crow-nose of the Idiot Childs!

HAVELOCK: Yes. It *is* good for me – and it's not 'childs', you cretin. Is it? It certainly ain't 'childs'.

ELLIS: So ... you just *know* what time we are. In the ... the pitch black. In*doors*. No light. *In*side. When you didn't even know what year. (*pause*) Y're lookin' forward to the Euros, are ye? That Gascoigne's looking fresh.

HAVELOCK: The year's irrelevant. When you're this ... when you're ... when you're in here.

ELLIS: So. Tell me that for starters at *least*. What are we, AM or PM? For the *aperitif* of our *illuminating* conversation. Shutters go up, or shutters stay down? What are we. Open for business – or closed for good – for good, forever? (*pause*) What'll it be?

ELLIS *begins to tick like the metronome.*

The clock is ticking. (*pause, aside*) Tick tock. (*looking down at the clock*) Or perhaps not, as the case may be. (*pause*) Well? (*pause*)

Look, Hal: I'm just trying to *manage* your expectations. It's not like it matters annyhow. Be this time tomorrow you're out on your arse. And me too. And back to – thieving from Percy Ingle's. (*pause*) Or's it beggin' be Barclays now. (*pause*) Out on our arses again, aye. At least that's something to be looking forward tae – 'cause it's the last I'll have to see of you!

HAVELOCK: Now don't you say that. You don't know that to-morrow's … you know, you don't know that. Don't say that. You can't.

ELLIS (*slowly*): Well isn't it *time* we opened up annyhow?

HAVELOCK (*confused*): Erm.

ELLIS (*chuckles*): Open the shutters will ye! (*saunters toward another of the shelves and rests an elbow*) Business hours have long since commenced, my dear Havelock, have they not? Sure look at all the monies we've missed out on already – all this *valuable* shite. (*gesturing around at the miscellany*) And someone'll come to buy it. Mark the words of me. We might even have enough here to save the whole fecking operation, not to mention all the starving wee Africans! And their oul' babies! Wouldn't that be grand, sure? (*pause*) And if we're to keep your precious palace afloat (*opens arms around him*) – we'd better get a move on, hadn't we? Shifting all of these … *treasures*. (*pause*) Starting with your fecked watch.

ELLIS *goes over to the display cabinet beside the till, flicks on another lamp, staring in at the watches.*

HAVELOCK: Well the clock's a write-off. An' that's your fault that. So go, go on then. It's *your* blasted turn to raise the shutters. (*agitated*) Get the key, would you … and … I thought it was for the elderly, this place? There're no Africans involved at all.

ELLIS: Pay no mind whose turn it is or what the feckin' *cause* is. *You* bring the beggars up. (*sitting down*) It's *your* thing, this. I've no interest in any of it. None at all. I'd as soon leave it be and find a place new. Start afresh, like – after you came in and bolloxed it up annyways. (*pause*) Sure isn't there annything more for me in this pissing life than picking me hole in a manky little charity shop – with the likes of you for company!

HAVELOCK: This is our home, El! This is where we kip, where we eat, you know and –

ELLIS: Aye, and fight – and shite!

HAVELOCK: Home!

ELLIS: It *is* not, ya big eej!

HAVELOCK: Everyone needs a reg'lar place to poo.

ELLIS: We're feckin' homeless, Hal! Homeless fellas don't have homes. That's kind of the defining characteristic, like. The sole criteria.

ELLIS *moves away from cabinet, absentmindedly toys with items around him.*

HAVELOCK: Isn't it all we have. And there's all sorts that'll happen yet – that *can* happen – 'tween now and then. This *can* be *home.* (*turning away*) You know well what Sophia said – so now I *know* you're just teasing. I get it. (*in a huff*) And that's, well, pretty damned cruel of you, Ellis.

ELLIS (*pause*): Always carrying on. Like an oul' biddy y'are.

HAVELOCK: You know what Sophia said.

ELLIS: Aye, aye. I know what she was after saying.

HAVELOCK: Right. All kinds of financial hoops to jump through. (*turning back*) Papers to be drawn up. Signed. All that. Surveys to be ... surveyed. Offers to be, you know what I mean. (*looks him up and down*) Well maybe you don't – but *deals to be done.* It isn't a quick snap of the fingers that a place like this gets sold. So why don't we spruce the place up a bit ... a big day ahead of us we have here.

ELLIS *begins his retort but simply grunts.*

HAVELOCK (*not listening, picking up hat*): Clean it up, you know, a little spit polish (*gestures around, smiling*), keep the place – y'know (*pauses, looking around at the general squalor*) – *of a standard.*

ELLIS (*to himself*): He keeps going. (*louder*) Of a standard, aye. Those were the words.

HAVELOCK: Then we'd be fine, stay on, no trouble. (*wiping spit out of hat with handkerchief*) Help get the thing back on its feet. Get *us* back on our feet.

ELLIS (*bored*): Back on our feet. That's what she said, aye.

HAVELOCK: Yes. Look. Y'know. Maybe they'll change their minds, these people? You said you seen 'em. Soft. City types, you said. We just ... put them off, a little. Then more ... *complications.* You know. And they give up!

ELLIS: What are ye yapping on about now? Like a mongoloid dog wi' a bone you are, give you half a chance.

HAVELOCK: Stranger things have happened, are happening – *will* happen. (*assuring*) We do the business here, you know, get back on our feet, you and I. What more can they ask for? Could make a real go of it here, us two. And we are the elderly after all!

ELLIS: A good kip on the couch. Aye. That's all I'm needing. (*pause, thinking*) That was a biteen weird, wasn't it? Calling them couches. Is that what she meant?

HAVELOCK: She meant chairs, I suppose. It's a minor point.

ELLIS: Aye, they're more an armchair than a settee. (*pause*) *Couch*. That's an odd word for *that*.

HAVELOCK: We'd have our meals in. No more ... crouching ... in the rain. Whatever we'd got together for the night, you know, we'd share it. That sorta' thing.

ELLIS: Aye, munching other fellas' sammiches. That sorta' thing.

HAVELOCK: Yes, other f... no. (*returning to his pontificating*) Just as long we kept it hush-hush, *on the down low*, as Richey says. As long as we stick to the agreement. I think we'll be all right.

ELLIS (*not listening*): Innocent, homeless people's sammiches. (*looking at his nails*) Blameless fellas who've *nothin'* else but a chair for kipping on. I mean, who steals from the homeless? I mean really. It's just not on, Hal.

ELLIS *finds and takes up the nail clippers from the side table and starts kicking off his boots, grunting to self.*

HAVELOCK: And that was the agreement. And we've stuck to it. No messing, no tomdickin' about. We've stuck to it.

ELLIS: The agreement. (*kicks off cowboy boots and pulls off socks*) That's all well and good for you, but I didn't sign any dotty line. How can I trust a word from her? I've been there before. They never come through these good Samaritan types.

HAVELOCK: We *swore*. *She* swore. A ... um ... A verbal wh-adjamacallit, was what it was. Due to its *unconventional* nature, shall we say.

ELLIS: *Verbal* my feckin' arse. *You* swore. Sure I wasn't even there. You took the notion to volunteer yourself – I hadn't anny say. I was only after suppin' away at me soup, listenin' to Jimmy Phelan carryin' on about his dirty pictures and what not. (*begins clipping toe nails*) If I'd had a say, I would have had you off and fecked to find your own shack.

HAVELOCK: What else was I to do? We were in the same position, were we not? Hell, it wasn't as if you had any prior engagements. Any ... kin ... any *well-wishers* willing to help you.

ELLIS (*grumbles*): Her fecking moonface. Sophie feckin' ugly arse moonface. Little fat thingeen that she is.

HAVELOCK: Now that's a medical condition, that. (*pause*) And it's Sophi*a*. With an 'ah'. Not that she minds, you saying it wrong every time – which is quite rude, very rude, in fact, very inconsiderate – no, she's not like that. She doesn't pay you no mind. And she's all the sweeter for it.

ELLIS: Face the size, shape and feckin' complexion of the moon – you're telling *me* it's medical, Dr Havelock.

HAVELOCK: Obese in the face. It's nothing to sniff at. That's Cushing's.

ELLIS: Cushions, aye. They'd help. Tape a few o' those to her head.

HAVELOCK: Cushing's. It's a *disease* ... or is it a syndrome. (*pause, goes to look up in a dictionary*) She's been nothing but a star, Ellis. Could you not show a little common decency. All she's done for us already. (*pause*) And after Edie.

ELLIS: Common decency, aye. Except it isn't all that decent, is it. (*thinking*) But aye, she's the friendly type, I'll grant you that. The harmless pushover kind, y'know. Simpling. A little bit dim, maybe. Sure didn't it only take a few flutters of your bushy eyelashes to get yourself holed up in here. Ye' thievin' git, ye'.

HAVELOCK (*pause*): Hm. Well I'm glad you can at least admit that much. That she's been good to us. She has. Always knew she was a good one. I know, we never met – before the ... visits. But I *knew*, you know? That she was one of the good ones?

ELLIS: And look where that's got us. Dangling a nice, warm ... cosy ... warm ...

HAVELOCK: You said warm.

ELLIS: ... place front of us. For all of what – a month, two months, however long. And then snatching it all away.

HAVELOCK: It's out of her hands. How was she to know. She only takes orders from the up-aboves. (*pause*) We're not even supposed to be here.

ELLIS (*pause*): You mean generally?

HAVELOCK (*continuing*): F'we put these young 'uns off, this couple, the ones you seen come for another mooch about the other week.

ELLIS: What'll you do? Take a shite in the cellar?

HAVELOCK: Oh I've got ideas.

ELLIS: Peggin' a poo up the stairs then. I don't think that'll cut it, like.

HAVELOCK (*pause*): No, not that.

ELLIS: What then? What feck-brained idea is it this time? Beyond selling enough doilies and feckin' Denby – and that we can somehow reverse the ... the centuries-long oppression of the ... the man on foot.

Long pause.

HAVELOCK: Well, how much can this place be worth?

ELLIS (*pause*): What's your point?

HAVELOCK: Decent enough location. (*looks around*) Tidy. *Ish.* How much you reckon?

ELLIS: To buy? Outright?

HAVELOCK: Well, yes. To buy. What is it.

ELLIS: Well. You could be looking at. Considering the location.

HAVELOCK: Yes?

ELLIS: For the lease, minimum six figures annual. Give or take. To buy ... not even worth thinkin' about. Why?

HAVELOCK (*thinking*): And what happens to the property if someone, you know ...

ELLIS: What.

HAVELOCK: Well. Croaks it.

ELLIS: What?

HAVELOCK: You know. If someone ... (*gestures up*) up and dies. In the downstairs or whatever.

ELLIS: Why the downstairs?

HAVELOCK (*pause*): Just because.

ELLIS: Think a death in the downstairs is not *quite* as bad, to be honest. *Stigmatised* property — is what they call it. Y'often hear of people dying in basements, don't ye? It mustn't be entirely unexpected to meet yir maker. Down there. In the basement. (*growing paranoid*)

HAVELOCK: Is it not?

ELLIS: In a way. (*pause*) And wouldn't *you* know about all'a this annyway?

HAVELOCK: And anywhere else? Ground floor? How's that figure into it? Y'know. A body on the ground level.

ELLIS: Well. That'd drop the price a fair bit now, probably — depending on the circumstances. And if annyone would be after tellin' ye'. And annyway. It'll be a place of business. No one cares if someone up and dies in a place of business. Happening every day, so it is. Sure look at that fella fell asleep c'lapsed into the fryer at Wimpy's. Deep fried half his face so he did. No one batted an eye. (*pause*) Well he sure didn't. Not after, like. Battered maybe.

HAVELOCK: How much would it be then?

ELLIS: I don't know! It'd drop the price, aye, but not be much, not really. People nowadays. Death's just part of the climate — along with us, like.

HAVELOCK: These lot'd be more concerned about the dead bodies and that, you'd think. With the, you know, the *negative energy*. You said they seemed the types, no?

ELLIS: Maybe. Why?

HAVELOCK: That'd put off-putting, wouldn't it? I mean, people would be put off, a fella dies, fella gets cut up into little bits, you know, an old boy's kicked down the stairs.

ELLIS: Yes, I suppose it would. Where's this going?

HAVELOCK (*pause*): No, nowhere in particular. Just, you know, thinking out loud.

ELLIS (*suspiciously*): What've you got planned? You don't go starting talk about people murdered in basements and kicked down stairs, then just go changing the subject quick as a flash.

HAVELOCK *gets behind the till.*

HAVELOCK: Changing what subject? We'd better hop to – sorting this mess, hadn't we?

ELLIS: Aye. Or it'll be more gob on that little turtley head of yours. (*waving clippers*) Or a clip around the ear.

HAVELOCK: Fine. (*opening the till*) There's no use arguing with a ... (*thinks better of hurling insults, sighs*). Even though you know very well I did it yesterday. And the day before. Look, you go get us some sangwidges.

Pause.

ELLIS: ... (*irritated, remembering*) I amn't going out *there* now! And for sammiches for the likes of you! (*pause*) And what did ya' mean exactly before: *idiot child*?

HAVELOCK: What's that?

ELLIS: I mean you, callin' me idiot child – (**HAVELOCK** *starts preparing the room, collecting up odd items and dropping them in a box*) Is it you mean that all childs are idiots, like? Or that I'm like a child what's an idiot, you know, just the one idiot child?

HAVELOCK: I don't have the foggiest what you're nattering on about.

ELLIS: It's just when you say these things, Hal. You know, they're ...

HAVELOCK: I mean. You just sit there while I do all the clearing, day in, day out. *And* me doing all the tidying, the cleaning – the what have you. Moving things to the basement. (*long pause*) I'm not the one who hasn't been pulling his weight, that's for sure.

Pause. **HAVELOCK** *walks over to and slumps into his chair. He gloomily drops a final item in the cardboard box, then stands there.*

ELLIS: Hey, now. (*finishes clipping toe nails*) Don't go starting with that carry on, now. Going all psycho on us again. I'll have to call the nurses for ye.

HAVELOCK: Mind your own. You ... Maybe I'll just put you in the basement.

ELLIS: Not if I put you there first.

HAVELOCK: You ... (*resigned*) This. The whole thing to rest.

Long pause.

ELLIS: Aye. (*pause*) Like the wife.

HAVELOCK: What?

ELLIS: The wife. Your wife. Put it to rest, I said. Like your wife, I was referring to.

HAVELOCK (*looks to* **HAVELOCK**, *pause, mumbling*): Yes, Edie.

ELLIS: Your wife what up and died. Aye. That was a sorry business so it was. That's what you're thinking about now, isn't it? The wife dying. (*putting his socks and boots back on*) I suppose it is. After me goin' mentionin' it there repeatedly.

HAVELOCK: Yes.

ELLIS: The way she just up and died on ya' like that. No word or annything. Or do you say 'passing' for that now, I'm not quite sure. And then you losing it, like. Sure that was just heaping tragedy on misery. (*Pause.*) Away and into the loony bin they sent you, wasn't it. When you couldn't handle, what was it, *the strain* of it all. Last straw an' all that guff.

HAVELOCK: They don't call it that anymore.

ELLIS: Don't call what what annymore?

HAVELOCK: Loony bin.

ELLIS: Sure I know that – they never did call it that, did they? That'd be awful feckin' insensitive. And that sort of carry on wouldn't be very helpful to annyone now, would it? (*pause*) The loony bin. Or 'the Funny Farm' which I always liked. That'd be just as bad, if not a biteen worse, like. Though I'm not sure where I heard that one. Or why it's worse actually.

HAVELOCK: Insensitive. That's what *you* are. Not to mention pig-headed. I don't know why I bother trying with you at all. If I had it my way, you'd be out on your arse in a jiff.

ELLIS: A jiff? Sure, you've got no fecker else. Isn't that about the measure of it? And wasn't I here first? Had it all sorted before you came swanning in. (*pause*) Out on *my* arse, ya feck.

HAVELOCK: I'd as soon chat away with meself if I'm being quite honest.

ELLIS: Isn't that the carry on what landed you in the Funny Farm the first place, sure?

HAVELOCK: Can you please ... I was unwell.

ELLIS: Sure wouldn't 'was' imply you're better now, like? Y'know. In the past? 'Was'?

HAVELOCK: I *am. Better.*

ELLIS: An' I suppose you can just *tell*, can ya' now? Threatenin' me with murder a minute before, so you were, even if it was only kidding. (*pause*) Better. Ya just *know*, like, I'm sure. That you're *better*. Just the same's it's 12. 12 all the day long. 12. 12. A 12ey 12 ... 12.

HAVELOCK: *I* at least speak generally in a sane manner. *You* on the other hand ...

ELLIS: "I speak generally in a sane manner." Would you hear this one? ... 12. "And 12 it'll always be to me" – wasn't that what you were after saying. Hardly the mutterings of a stable mind now, are they?

HAVELOCK: I make ... sense. I do. You know I do.

ELLIS: Know you do what? More like the ramblings of a simpleton – one particularly dim baby one brained recently be a horse. (*pause*) You need help you do. Have a mind to call up them nurses right now, so I do. D'ye have the number handy?

HAVELOCK: Is that what you want, then? Is it?

ELLIS (*pause*): ... The Casserole ... Crazy House.

HAVELOCK: Listen to yourself going on, and on. And on. Do you not tire of that *sickening* gurgle of yours?

ELLIS: Sure, an' mad people aren't mad either now, are they? All just because they say they aren't. (*pause*) I mean, why, *for instance*, are ye still not rid of all that skitter below?

HAVELOCK: What's it to you? None of your damned business, is it?

ELLIS: Well it won't be me carrying it the next place, so it won't. Luggin' around some big feckin' box 'cause you can't just leave it behind, give it away, or sell it, or even open it! Or whatever it is you be doing to it. A box o' things kep' all sealed up. (*pause*) Donations, that was it. Donations, you said. But sealed you've left them. Kep' the key (*long pause*) Go fetch it, will I? That big treasure box thingeen. All sealed up like.

HAVELOCK: Do what you like. I'm not paying you any mind.

ELLIS *runs downstairs to grab the box. He talks all the while, before he brings it up.*

HAVELOCK (*quietly*): I still have the key.

ELLIS (*off*): You know. It's a deceptively heavy little thing, this. So it makes me very curious. Very very ... very curious indeed. Oh, and will I check the fridge, grab meself a little *sangwidge* too while I'm at it? I will. Oh, wait – no. I won't. Because some fat greedy fat fecker's gone ...

HAVELOCK: You said 'fat'.

ELLIS: ... and scoffed them all. Not only his, what I gave him ...

HAVELOCK: From the *donations* actually ...

ELLIS: ... but mine too!

HAVELOCK: Hmpf.

ELLIS: And have you left anny tobacco? No. (*pause*) And the feckin' back door's been left wide open too! Born in a feckin' barn, was he? Packed to the rafters wi' brained babies and mongoloid dogs!

HAVELOCK: Please.

ELLIS (*appearing, holding box*): Gwan', we'll just have a little lookeen.

ELLIS *drops the box in the middle of the room with a thump.*

HAVELOCK: Ellis. Please. Not this again.

ELLIS: A quick peep. (*short pause.*) Tell me. What's it they found you at – I mean, when they finally locked ya up for being a mental?

HAVELOCK (*turning*): You know very well the conditions of my ... hospitalisation. What happened. (*getting up, struggling*) Sophia, she'll not be long. Put that way now. Please. She'll be here soon. We haven't the time nor need for this.

ELLIS: But of course, of course. What am I at? It's openin'-up time, isn't it? Or isn't it. I'm just trying to manage your expectations either way, y'know. Let's do this: the box or the shutters – you choose.

HAVELOCK *walks over and picks up the clock, handles it. Turns the hands round with his finger. Twirling the minute hand anti-clockwise.* **ELLIS** *lifts the box, carries it smirking back downstairs.*

HAVELOCK: Privacy. Just some privacy is all I need. All anyone needs. Privacy ...

ELLIS (*calling*): Privacy! No ...

HAVELOCK: And a bit of common decency, but constantly ... under the microscope ...

ELLIS (*appearing again*): Decency! Ha! You're damned right – *under the microscope* is where ya' should be ... (*pause*) Wonder of feckin' science that y'are. Clutchin' a stinkin', rottin' corpse all wrapped up like a pig in a blanket – Dad's Army on, probably. (*sneaks up to* HAVELOCK) Aye, a stinking, rotten sack of bones. *Decent privacy's* what *you* were at. (*pause*) Y'know, not *everyone* can be trusted wi' that. Prime feckin' example, you are. I mean, you see that yourself, surely. A bunch of youse out running wild ... Knivin', rapin' – thievin' sammiches – proper mental stuff. That'd be mayhem sure ... And putting the undertakers out of a job fr'another one. (*longer pause*)

No. That's exactly why there can'n't be no privacy for the likes of you. Can'n't be no trust.

ELLIS *produces an apple from his hoodie, rubs it, takes a big crunching bite.*

HAVELOCK (*morosely*): Why? Who says? You? I wanted ... only to ... keep her. With me. Up here. A little while longer. You can't be ready, how can you be? She was ... But I ... (*long pause*) I mean, why throw her under ... why ... (*trails off*).

ELLIS: Oh here it comes again. All aboard the loony train. (*bites apple*) Toot toot.

HAVELOCK (*louder*): Why cast her into the ground? So soon. She ... never asked for that.

ELLIS: ... No one does! It's not something you need to ask for! (*pause*) Oh, aye. Will ye bury me or burn me when I go, ya' will?

Thanks, like. (*pause*) Why bury her? Christ. I can only assume you *can'n't* hear yourself when you say these things. (*pause*) And "I speak generally in a sane manner," says he.

HAVELOCK: Just to keep her with me, a little longer. (*pause, almost in tears*) So's I don't forget her. I couldn't bear to forget that ... smile.

ELLIS: Sure, you'd ne'er forget an experience like that in a hurry, would ye. Aye. No privacy for the likes of you – because we *haven't a clue* what you *mentals* 're up to. The sheer *imagination* on you feckers. It boggles the mind, it really does. Keepin' her months – behind the feckin' settee! Brilliant! Or was it a couch?

HAVELOCK: It does no harm. Did no harm. Why do *they* get to take her –

ELLIS: Sure, what's the sausage roll without the meat, like? Not to mention *flat out* agin' the *law*. You know. Real basic stuff, like. And I've not even mentioned whore-y neither.

HAVELOCK: And abiding the whore of Lady Justice is what's brought you here, sleeping upright in a spastics' society sofa —

ELLIS: —chair

HAVELOCK: —not even good enough for spastics. Yeeesss. That's the ticket. Mr. Bumbling Fucking Law Abiding Idiot. (*mumbling*) And yet he doesn't answer the question.

ELLIS: Ey?

HAVELOCK: Nothing.

ELLIS: No, say that again. What you said there about the question – what question?

HAVELOCK (*pause*): What can you give a man who has nothing?

ELLIS *shakes his head.*

ELLIS: 20 quid would be a decent start. I've a mind to give Willy Wonka a tinkle right now so I do. Have 'em swing by, pop you in the Funny wagon. You're losin' it, fella ... Or have you just *found* it? (*beat*) Now, how's that for a question.

Long pause.

So it was ... only you and her when they came in. (*quizzically*) What's it you were up to?

HAVELOCK (*indignant*): What are you getting at?

ELLIS: What'd you done with her, like? Where were ye?

HAVELOCK: In the living room – I don't understand.

ELLIS (*menacingly*): In the living room. You – and that corpse.

HAVELOCK: My wife. She wasn't a *corpse*. Isn't a *corpse*. She's my wife. My wife, Edie.

ELLIS: Aye, the wife. The encircled corpse. And you hadn't been dressing her up, I suppose, no. Setting the table an' that, feeding her the tea and mashed-up biscuits and what have you. Feeding her stole sammiches. You know, of an evening. None of that malarkey I suppose.

HAVELOCK: ... No.

ELLIS: Puppetin' the jaw and talkin' with it, like – like she's yappin' away atcha' still. Talkin' the hind legs off ... well, her ... self.

HAVELOCK: No.

ELLIS: Did ye' think of shufflin' her 'long the floor like a broom, walking like? Did you even think of that one? I'd be surprised if you didn't. I'd expect you, being a mental and all, might come up with something *good* to do with her, like. While you're at it.

HAVELOCK: No.

ELLIS: In the bath? Had her in the bath, no?

HAVELOCK: Please.

ELLIS: You know, scrubbing her up clean as a whistle for a night on the tiles. (*pause*) The bathroom tiles. Arms sloshin' about like a fish. Mouth of red lippy and the bubbles.

HAVELOCK: No. But if I had – clothed her, I mean – well that wouldn't be anything out of the ordinary. As far as convention goes, that's the very least of what occurs when the authorities get their hands on you. Then it's anyone's guess.

ELLIS: There isn't much convention to what ye were at. *Convention.*

HAVELOCK: ... I'll have you know – there are far more places than you'd think where that's not at all out of the ordinary. Not at all strange. Look. (*begins searching for a particular book*)

ELLIS: But you're not in anny o' those *mad's a shitting bollock* places. Are ye'? (*pause*) And all of it punishable be common law to boot. But you'd know that wouldn't you. Ending up the dock as you did. When all it was was a little formeen that needed filling. Maybe a ... courtesy call on the blower. (*pause*) It's just unprofessional behaviour – not management material.

HAVELOCK: Yes.

ELLIS: I mean, five days is what they're already giving ye. God knows five days is plenty to get out outta' the way whatever it was ye' had in mind. I mean, ye' were just greedy. Months ye' were at it! (*pause*) And ye' haven't anny of the pictures now, would ye?

HAVELOCK (*pause*): No. I didn't think of a camera. Wasn't *top of mind* then.

ELLIS: Top of mind. You see most people, they want to *remember* something, you know what it is they do? They get out the oul' camera. You know. Or like little Richey with his yoke, forever snappin' away so he is. (*pause*) Photographic evidence'd only make matters worse, I s'pose though, aye. You'd have to do one of those — what's it they call it — them things?

HAVELOCK: Haven't a clue.

ELLIS (*low*): A selfie, aye. With the wife. "Here's me, the wife our feet up, out the back garden." (*thinking*) Ye' had a garden, didn't ye'. (*pause*) "Here's me, the wife, and her spread across the kitchen table so she is. Head in the bread bin." (*almost trembling with excitement*) She must have been a right state — and I'm guessing hasn't recovered since.

HAVELOCK (*ignoring* ELLIS, *picking a book out from shelf*): Look: here. Ancient burial rituals in this one. Read it there for yourself.

ELLIS: Ow, not that feckin' whatcha' call him again. (*pause*) Sophocles [*pronounced: 'Soff-ocles', rhymes with 'monocles'*]. (*pause*) Not him. So shite they named him the once.

HAVELOCK (*learnedly, almost to himself*): Mononymity wasn't uncommon in those days. (*pause*) And no, it's not *Sophocles*. It's … (*looking*) it's the Kingfisher Encyclopaedia of Geography actually.

ELLIS: Momomimmity – what?

HAVELOCK: *Mononymity*. One name. You *are* dim sometimes. And there's only one name for what you are and all.

ELLIS: One name. Aye, like that fella.

HAVELOCK: Who. (*still searching through book*)

ELLIS: Aye, *Seal*. Aye, gobshites, mainly. Sophocles. Plato [*pronounced*: Play-Doh]. JohnBonJovi. (*pause*) The gobshites that do be piling up there (*points at books and CDs*) and can't be shifted for love nor wealth. (*pause*) Sting's another one of the fecks. Don't even get me started on that mope. Who else.

HAVELOCK (*searching through book*): Africa. Indochina. See? And that's before we even get to embalming.

ELLIS: Savages. Savages the lot. (*pause*) Oh and Björk!

HAVELOCK: Rather sophisticated for savages ...

ELLIS: Sure weren't they at cuttin the little heads off babies so the sun wouldn't go out?

HAVELOCK: Björk?

ELLIS: The Chinesians.

HAVELOCK: Whoever told you that?

ELLIS: Aye, wasn't it Richey who was after telling us the one day. From his lessons. In the colleges. And that they squish them into little edible bite-sized thingeens. That's what he was after telling us. And sell them be the side of the roads.

HAVELOCK (*flicking erratically through pages*): I can't find it now. It's here somewhere.

ELLIS: Annyway. You hadn't dressed her up like, the wife in her best undies.

HAVELOCK (*looking up*): I did change her clothes on occasion, yes. You start to see stains, you see.

ELLIS *makes a face.*

HAVELOCK: But not for *that.*

ELLIS (*letting his imagination run wild, begins to roam the room, fancifully teasing* HAVELOCK): Or did ye put on the lippy?

HAVELOCK (*following him with his eyes*): Or ... no.

ELLIS (*stops, facing away, menacingly*): Or have a little peek.

HAVELOCK *momentarily gags but says nothing. He reaches out for the picnic knife but can't quite reach, so closes the book.*

ELLIS: Or a little play.

HAVELOCK: Look – show some god-damned respect will you.

ELLIS: Aye, aye.

Long pause.

So it wasn't the last go on her then, no, was it? One last hurrah. (*Short pause*) One final blast of the cannon, like.

HAVELOCK (*snatching up the knife,* HAVELOCK *strides over to* ELLIS *and stands there, looming, holding the picnic knife behind his back*): Look, now.

ELLIS (*confrontationally*): And what are *you* at? A bit of looming is it now? (*pause*) Don't be going looming over me. Ye' with yer' gobby hat. I'll lay you out, boyo.

HAVELOCK: All I did was hold her. (*numbly, throws down knife*) Cradle her fragile, bony frame (*cradles his arms loosely, slowly raising them to his chest, then temples*) hold her to me, tight in my arms (*pause*) and carry her to our bed. (**HAVELOCK** *walks away slowly, holding his head. Takes a seat*)

ELLIS: ... That isn't what you told the guards now, was it? And the doctors with it? That you were after taking her to bed after all?

HAVELOCK: To lay her down into sleep.

ELLIS: Lay her down into what was that?

HAVELOCK *is silent. Pause.*

ELLIS (*thinking*): Hold on. Hold on. Ye' were after saying living room before? Ye' said in the living room it was ye' had her – I mean not had her had her, you know, had her – as in had her sat in there with ya' gassin' on the settee.

HAVELOCK: Yes. What.

ELLIS: So you did take her to bed? Or you moved her or what. Up the stairs. Or was it one of the bungaloweens ye' had, special made for oul' dyin' fellas.

HAVELOCK: Can you get to the point?

ELLIS: Sure it doesn't add up so it doesn't. You said you didn't touch her. And now she's in the bedroom. When first it was the living room.

HAVELOCK (*short pause*): The bedroom was the living room. The bed was in the living room.

ELLIS: Oh. (*pause*) I see. Well that would explain that. (*pause, watches* HAVELOCK *suspiciously*) But it's an altogether peculiar arrangement that, so it is.

HAVELOCK: Mm.

ELLIS: Ye were hardly the conventional sorts no, be the sounds o' things. (*pause*) Aye. You didn't often have guests over for tea, I'd wager? Altogether weird goings-on around your house.

Long pause.

HAVELOCK: She'll be here soon. Better get to the cleaning.

ELLIS: Aye. Back to *that* so it is – your cleaning, and forgetting that you've eaten my *blasted* breakfast.

ELLIS *lolls around the bookshelf pondering.* **HAVELOCK** *sits on the edge of the chair, the majority of the tidying done.* **HAVELOCK** *shifts in his seat.* **ELLIS** *rounds the shelf and leans forward, poking his head almost through the gap, staring menacingly at* **HAVELOCK**.

HAVELOCK *innocently raises his finger slowly, his sleeve pulling back again. As he lifts it up, he glances at his wrist, thinking again that he has a watch – he has forgotten it's in the cabinet.*

HAVELOCK: El, I want to ask you something. (*pause*) Was it ever suicide you considered? Have you, you know … thought about it. You know.

ELLIS: Where's this from, all of a sudden.

HAVELOCK: The life you've led.

ELLIS: What's that supposed to mean?

HAVELOCK: I mean. In your situation, you know, before. It'd be no surprise, you know. No beggar would second guess ya', lad. The life you've had.

ELLIS: Why would I — I had it made before you turned up. *Arse*.

HAVELOCK: It'd be normal.

ELLIS: You're goin' telling me what's normal then, are ye?

HAVELOCK: No. Well. I suppose we don't know 'bout that.

ELLIS: Would Sophia like to know more about *your* past? What do you think?

Long pause.

HAVELOCK (*suddenly*): Breakfast! Ah-ha!

ELLIS: Aye you've it eaten sure. What? (*removes his head from the bookshelf's empty square*)

HAVELOCK: You said breakfast. You just said *breakfast*. So it *is* morning!

ELLIS: Breakfast breakfast. So? (*turns his back*)

HAVELOCK: *So* you said *breakfast*. I knew it! The sangwidge was for *breakfast*. It's morning! A-ha!

ELLIS: And?

HAVELOCK: And well. Yes. (*realising*) Christ! (*pause*) Then this is it ...

ELLIS *begins eyeing the watches in the cabinet. Picks up* **HAVELOCK**'s *watch.*

HAVELOCK: I'm not ashamed. Nothing to be ashamed of. Idiot! Now help with this would ya. If it's breakfast then it's morning – and if it's morning, it's opening-up time.

HAVELOCK *moves across to a bowl of keys and begins searching. He takes one and starts turning the key in the lock.* **ELLIS** *moves to help lift it from beneath. By the end they speak over each other frantically, both exasperated by their squabbling.*

ELLIS: What were ye so? A coward? Too yella' to face the music.

HAVELOCK (*incredulous*): Just lift it would you. Too yella' ... It takes guts to do what I did for her.

ELLIS: Aye – too yella' to face the music is what I'm after saying. Before you went ahead ...

HAVELOCK: Gibberish is all it is. Your mouth (*pause*) What is it you've done in your mangey life – on the street, I might add – that's so damned – so damned honourable – towering fecking paragon of human valour that you are, hoarding secret sangwidges and apples. Yes. Sangwidges and apples. I've seen you.

ELLIS: Apples now you've got a problem with, is it?

HAVELOCK: Apples, sangwidges. Satsumas – oh, and crackers.

ELLIS: Is what *you* are! Ha!

HAVELOCK: Crackers – your crunchy little friends. Feeble is what they make you. Feeble *and* fat.

ELLIS: What crackers?

HAVELOCK: The crackers that you're forever munching away at. The Jacobs. (*pause*) Those crackers!

ELLIS: The apples and the sangwidges and the crackers. Simple tastes I must have when they're totted out like that in a list, like.

HAVELOCK: Well. Simple tastes for a simpling mind. Now if they were *Ritz* crackers ...

ELLIS (*interrupting*): Simpling is it?

HAVELOCK: Yes. As opposed to middling.

HAVELOCK *gets down and fetches another set of keys.*

ELLIS (*pause*): Well – wait a minute. Wouldn't the opposite now – would that not be doubling, so?

HAVELOCK: Em. Well I couldn't say.

HAVELOCK *tries new keys.*

ELLIS: Have you there now I do – because maths aren't your strong point I know for a fact. (*pause*) Or is it nothing. The opposite to middling now. Nothing, would it be?

HAVELOCK: This serves only to illustrate my point.

ELLIS: And anyway. I've done many the more honourable deed than *yourself.* Heaps more I might add. (*snide*) Mr. High and Mighty. Things that made *a difference* to real folk. Their *lives.* A turf load more'n you. Never minding your *lah-di-dah* skitter. No, you'll never know me. I'm as unknowable to ye' as ... as rain – like a cloud followin' ye', watchin'. That one and only rain drop that starts 'em all.

HAVELOCK (*growing more incredulous*): *You? Honourable,* like what?

ELLIS: Well. If it's a list we're at. Letting you in here, for one. Letting you stay. There's one. And alive. Well looked-after, even. That'd be the first to make me list. The opening gambit, like.

HAVELOCK: Christ – is that *still* the issue?

ELLIS (*stops trying to life the shutters, stands gesticulating*): You bet your fecking wrinkly hole it's still the issue! You know well it's the feckin' issue!

HAVELOCK (*unthinking*): Will he ever give it a rest? Like a dog with a bone he is.

ELLIS: Don't go changing the subject on us – to bones and mongoloids of all things. Still the issue is what I'm saying.

HAVELOCK: Oh, come on. Now I'm curious. Tell me what it is you've *ever* done – for *anyone* – that was *ever* honourable?

ELLIS: ... (*pause*) Look, Havelock. (*thoughtfully*) There are ... simply *things* that are beyond the understanding of men like you. Weak of mind. Sore of heart. The coward that couldn't face up t'is wife dying. Couldn't ... face the truth of it. Instead, gone and locked up in a loony bin!

HAVELOCK: Face it? You know nothing about it! So go on then. What've you done? Do tell.

ELLIS (*pause, starts lifting again*): One way to tell a decent man from another is – he always asks *one* question. It mightn't be delivered in always – always the gentlest of fashions – but any man of any measure puts it forward.

HAVELOCK: And? What is it?

ELLIS: See. You've never asked it. (*pause*) I thought you were goin' t' earlier, but ya' don't have it in you. So I know about you. Even if *you* don't know about yoursel'.

HAVELOCK (*pause*): Well, actually, come to think of it – no. I don't think I ever have asked. I kind of just assumed, y'know. You seem the type.

ELLIS: The type?

HAVELOCK (*goes back to trying keys*): You have that kind of look about you.

ELLIS (*stops lifting*): What *look*?

HAVELOCK: Rough-looking. Homeless, like.

ELLIS: With a little hobo hamper, is it? A little feckin' bindle stick and a hamper with me little sammiches and apples. Is that what ye think?

HAVELOCK: And your *crackers*.

ELLIS: Well. You're just the fecking same as the rest of them you are. I've got *integrity* at least. Dignity. Because do you know what – *naw* ...

HAVELOCK: I don't know if you've taken a look in the mirror lately, El. Integrity and dignity aren't exactly the first two words that'd spring to mind.

ELLIS: And what'd those words be then. (*pause*) Ye' soft shite.

HAVELOCK (*sarcastic/offensive Irish accent*): Let me have a thin-keen. Tesco ham sammiches in the one fist. And a fistful of toe nail clippings in the other. Ye' potato.

ELLIS: Are ye' finished with y'ir xenophobic rant? You have no real, proper criteria for what makes a *true* man, so?

HAVELOCK: A *true* man? You think *you're* a *true* man?

ELLIS: A truer man than you – aye, certainly.

HAVELOCK (*long pause*): Yes, this is – I'm waiting. For the proof.

ELLIS: I wouldn't tell a gobshite like you. You're 100% the type that can not *under no circumstances* be trusted. Ultimately. I mean (*pause*) If only I *had* met her first.

HAVELOCK: Then what is it you think would've happened?

ELLIS: I think we both know.

HAVELOCK: The handsome hobo swoops in? Crackers for dinner?

There's a sudden and loud rapping at the shutters. They drop silent and hide. Long pause.

ELLIS: Shhhh! (*pause, looking at* **HAVELOCK**) What are ye hidin' for? The feckin' shutters are down. No one can see ye, ye coward.

HAVELOCK (*whispering*): Shush yourself. Don't think I don't see you whimpering there in the Jamie Olivers. (*pause*)

The rapping again, louder.

What *is* that? (*pause*) Sophia has a key (*sneaks over to a rota pinned to the wall*) And no one else is due in this week. (*to himself*) It's the last week. The first week – of the year. Why would ...

ELLIS: Shush! Listen!

More rapping.

HAVELOCK: Shush, will you?

They listen. Pause. There's a murmured shout of "Open up!" The rapping gets louder before another pause. We wait. Then one final BANG.

HAVELOCK: Christ. Sounds like the heaven's are openin' up out there. And you, all the rain's in here!

ELLIS: They really meant that, I think.

HAVELOCK: Who? What? What do they want? Give yourself up, Ellis. If it's something you've gone and done it's only fair on the rest of us. Don't go dragging the ship down with the crew. You're always ... settin' fire to postboxes or whatever it is ye' be getting' up tae.

ELLIS: Hush you! With your xenophobia – *again.*

HAVELOCK: But what if it's, y'know, *them* – to boot us out already? What if the deal's gone through? We'll be ... out on the street. (*dismal*) By ... lunchtime?

ELLIS: Just stay put.

Both men lean towards the door to listen. They lean in closer, hearing something.

ELLIS: Are you hearing that?

HAVELOCK: What?

Long pause.

ELLIS: Something ... (*short pause*) walking.

A figure sneaks in rear doorway seen by the audience, a silhouette moving across the stage in the darkness.

HAVELOCK: That'd probably be the sound of your bolloxed brain departing.

RICHEY (*entering, then very loud, switching on light*): HAPPY NEW YEAR, FUCKERS!

The men yelp and jump into each other's arms, falling backwards into **ELLIS**'s *chair. Enter* **RICHEY**, *a somewhat scrawny youth with a trustworthy face. Wears a similar tracksuit to* **ELLIS**, *just without the price tags.* **RICHEY** *is dripping with rain.*

RICHEY (*laughing*): Why the fuck ain't you opened up? It's pissin' down out there.

HAVELOCK: Oh. Is it?

RICHEY: And don't you know what time it is, fellas? Just dozin' about with ya' dicks in ya' hands.

HAVELOCK *and* **ELLIS** *look to each other and back at* **RICHEY**. *They let go of one another,* **ELLIS** *stands, embarrassed.*

ELLIS: Ya' scrote ye'. Half near frightened the arsehole out of me.

RICHEY: Actually, yeah – I'm kinda' lucky you ain't both keeled over dead like. (*pause*) But it ain't my fault I gotta' let me self in now is it. An a right bitch gettin' that latch lifted an' all. Someone'd fuckin' double-locked it. Fire hazard for one.

ELLIS: Sure who breaks into charity shops?

RICHEY: I work 'ere, mate. I've got a key. That is the *exact opposite* of breakin' in.

RICHEY *begins drying himself off. He's drenched, takes off his hoody, hangs it on a bookshelf.*

ELLIS: Yeah, but aren't we the ones what live here? Ya' feckin' gob shite. A blatant invasion of our privacy is what that is!

RICHEY: Privacy? (*laughs*) You're *homeless* – what d'you need privacy for? (*pause*) Naw. I'm only messin'. Don't go cryin' now. (*laughs*) I thought you'd be all tucked up anyway, after a heavy night'a boozin' (*quietly*) or whatever is you two gay lords get up to in here.

ELLIS: What is it y're after, so? Moochin' about in the dark. (*to* **HAVELOCK**) The dark. Suits him, don't it?

RICHEY: I've just gotta' pick something up. Prick.

HAVELOCK: Hey. So what time *is* it then?

RICHEY *pauses and stares at watch, too long.*

HAVELOCK: Not you an' all.

RICHEY: Not me an' all, what? It's stopped. Must be the rain or summink'.

HAVELOCK: The time?

RICHEY *looks to the clock missing from the wall, finally sees the state of the room.*

RICHEY: Fuck me. What's occurred in 'ere? What've you done to the place? Looks like fuckin' Wotsit've bin.

HAVELOCK: Wha'?

RICHEY (*to* **ELLIS**): And what've *you* come as?

HAVELOCK (*growing agitated*): What's the damn *time*?!

ELLIS: We've tidied up grand, thank you very much. And you're welcome.

HAVELOCK: Is she coming now? Sophia? (*pause*) What's the time, god damnit?!

RICHEY: Oh. Nah lads. That's why I'm here. Sophia – Sophia ain't comin'.

The men glance at each other.

RICHEY: Need to tell you. (*pause, looking at watch*) Ah, it's started again. She's er (*pause*) She's been involved in an accident ... This weather an' everything.

HAVELOCK: She what?

ELLIS (*concerned*): What happened her?

RICHEY: A bus. It was ... er, the 462.

HAVELOCK (*delighted, to* ELLIS): A bus? A bus!

RICHEY: Smacked her clean out of her shoes.

HAVELOCK (to ELLIS): Smacked her clean! Where?

RICHEY: Flattened her mate.

HAVELOCK: And then flattened!

ELLIS: Christ. When?

HAVELOCK: And is it serious?

RICHEY: Mate – it was a bus.

HAVELOCK (*hopeful*): Then it *is*! Saved! We're saved!

ELLIS *steps over to* RICHEY.

ELLIS: Where is she? (*scrambling, gets his coat, also price tagged – puts it hurriedly over his tracksuit.*) Where did they take her?

RICHEY *steps across to the shutters, struggling to find the words. He quickly finds the right key and presses the button. The shutters start to come up.*

RICHEY (*cursing the shutters*): Christ's sake – these still not actin' right?

HAVELOCK *stands there, rubbing his arms – he goes to sit down. He's excited.* **ELLIS** *is in shock, moves slowly.*

ELLIS: Where did they take her? Where is she? Rich?

Pause.

RICHEY: She ain't nowhere now mate. (*pause, shutters stop momentarily*) She dead.

Shutters suddenly snap up, revealing a blinding shaft of sunlight that blinds them as the shutters rise. The men stand stunned. Blinding white light.

RICHEY: Now. That's better.

Blackout.

Act II
Scene One

Some time before Act I, HOPE *is open for business. The shop has been transformed and is in full flow. Music is playing, the shelves are packed, clothes rails full. Trinkets here and there are being eyed and handled by a smattering of interested shoppers, old and young, coming and going, spontaneously interacting with each other.*

ELLIS *can be seen among them, proudly moving about the shop, helping customers, readjusting merchandise. He moves gracefully as if on air.*

ELLIS *finishes his rounds and goes to stand behind the till again. He looks about contentedly. He sits and resumes reading his book which has been left butterflied on the worktop: a GCSE study book of a Sophocles collection (e.g.* Antigone*).*

The bell tinkles as the door opens. Enter **RICHEY** *checking his phone.* **ELLIS** *doesn't see him until he comes around the back of the till, eyeing vintage-styled girls and student-types, before slapping* **ELLIS** *on the shoulder.*

RICHEY: A'ight fucker?

Customers suddenly turn in mild shock to look, go back to their browsing.

What? Fuckin' ...

ELLIS (*happy to see him*): Aye, aye – and yourself? (*They shake hands vigorously*)

RICHEY: Not bad, mate, not bad. (*pause*) Sophia's still on me case though innit (*holds up phone*) – 'bout sortin' those boxes downstairs.

ELLIS: Well now, she *did* say a while ago, like.

RICHEY: Takin' her side, are ya'? I'm a fuckin' volunteer! You don't go tellin' fuckin' volunteers what to be doin' – I ain't being paid, bruv! Straight up exploitation's what it is.

ELLIS: Ha! Exploitation! That's a biteen over the top.

RICHEY: You *only* get the right to tell people what to do when you're payin' 'em.

ELLIS: Is that so, aye? And am I being paid, sure? Sure don't I follow the orders handed t'me, no questions. Swallee' the lot whole so I do. (*pause*) Do this, do that. Spruce up the window display. Rearrange the chairs and that. Sort the CDs – in alphabetical order, mind. I've no other choice, do I. (*pause*) Now. Pay no mind to all that carry on and get with it, would ya'? We're the lot of us volunteers, ye bogue.

RICHEY: Mate, you're cotchin' a fuckin' prime bit o' real estate 'ere – rent free, food – shitty Co-Op food but yeah, still food, jus' about. *And* you're *completely* on your jacks – more freedom than you should probably have really, if I'm honest. I'd consider *that* pay, mate. Basically a fuckin' bed and breakfast. (*pause, smiling*) Or's it a bit – a bit more like prison, El? Just with ... even less in the windows.

A young couple, well-dressed City-types FRANCIS *and* NADIA, *enters quietly –* ELLIS *and* RICHEY *continue their dispute. The couple look around, not at the items for sale but carefully at the interior's structure, use of space, paying close attention.*

ELLIS: Sophia doesn't be bringing me rashers and white puddin' of a mornin'. (*beat*) And sure I wouldn't know about the B&Bs.

RICHEY: Wouldn't you now? (*pause*)

ELLIS: And what are ye insinuating now?

RICHEY: Insinuating?

ELLIS: Lettin' on ye' know – somethin'.

RICHEY: What.

ELLIS: I don't take no handouts. This is work, lad. Work.

RICHEY: Look all I'm sayin' is, you *live* here, yeah? You're at least getting *something* out of it. What do I get? When we really look at it. A fucking Tesco sandwich an' a manky pack o' Space Raiders. If *that*. Don't appreciate bein' bossed 'bout by no one.

ELLIS: Now don't be forgettin' your little bottleen o' pink Fanta.

RICHEY: Yeah and me Fanta … *Red* Fanta. It ain't pink bruv.

ELLIS: And I mean – *y'are* on community service, like. It's generous enough they're bein' – 'cos you're a cursed little gobshite, truth be told. If *I'm* honest.

FRANCIS *leans in to interrupt just as* ELLIS *goes to speak.* ELLIS *and* RICHEY *look at him.*

ELLIS: Hullo?

RICHEY (*sarcastically*): Gwan. Can we *help* you fam?

FRANCIS *stutters and looks confusedly at his partner. She steps forward.*

NADIA: Nice to meet you. We're Mr and Mrs Wade. Here to meet Sophia? Sophia who manages the premises?

ELLIS: Sophia? She's er, she's popped out, I'm afraid. Not be in today. (*pause*) Sorry, what was it your name was again?

NADIA: Nadia.

RICHEY (*cutting in*): I'm afraid Nadia, she's been called away – a family emergency, yeah.

NADIA: Oh, I hope it's nothing serious?

RICHEY: Just a – barbecue.

FRANCIS: … An emergency *barbecue*?

RICHEY: Nah erm – not barbecue. What am I sayin'?

ELLIS: What *are* you saying? It's nothing, really – (*overly dramatic whisper*) her daughter's got the runs. (*pause*) A cold or something.

NADIA: Oh. That's a relief.

RICHEY: Isn't it. (*he leans in onto his elbows, creepily assessing her*) She'll be back fighting fit in no time.

NADIA: The runs, though – that doesn't sound like a cold at all. If I'm honest.

NADIA *stares back intimidatingly then dismissively, then looking around the room, assessing it still.* RICHEY *is slightly put off, but appears strangely attracted.*

RICHEY: I s'pose not.

ELLIS (*to* FRANCIS): And sorry, what is it they call you, sir? Have we met?

FRANCIS: Francis. It's Francis.

ELLIS: Ah, a Frank. I knew a Frank once.

FRANCIS: Nope, just good ol' Francis. *Old* school like that, y'see.

ELLIS (*continues, not listening*): A lovely fellow he was, Frank. Had a thing for – *what was it.* Commemorative neckerchiefs, I think. And those long curly-toed shoes that clowns do be wearin'.

FRANCIS: Right.

ELLIS: And do I detect an accent there, Frank?

FRANCIS: You do indeed.

ELLIS: Where is it ye hail from? Accents are my thing.

FRANCIS: Australia.

ELLIS (*not hearing/listening*): What is it? Oh no, let me guess first. Let's have a little stabeen at it.

FRANCIS *looks quizzically at* NADIA.

FRANCIS: Sure? Shoot.

RICHEY: Come *on.*

ELLIS: Now say that again, g'wan.

RICHEY: Ellis, please.

FRANCIS (*smiling*): But that's cheating?

NADIA: He's ... obviously ... Australian. He just said?

ELLIS *repeats* FRANCIS's *question back to him.*

ELLIS (*doing an accent*): 'Cheating'? Up, it goes up. 'Cheating'? Well now, that's Australian if I amn't mistaken.

FRANCIS (*now humouring him, polite*): Bang on, buddy. You've quite the ear. (*pause, glances to* **NADIA** *then back*) And yourself? I hear a little Irish lilt in there?

RICHEY (*thumbing to* **ELLIS**): 'im? He's Cockney. Can't you tell?

NADIA: That's what *I* would have said. Bit of a ... mixed-up accent.

ELLIS: Mixed up? Well – if I am or I amn't. It's been a whileen since I've set the old trotters back on the fair green soil ... a good long whileen.

RICHEY (*chuckling*): ... What *is* that accent even? (*to* **FRANCIS** *and* **NADIA**) He don't actually talk like that.

An awkward silence. **ELLIS** *drums his fingers on the counter.* **FRANCIS** *and* **NADIA** *confidently look them over.*

ELLIS: And what are you insinuating with that exactly?

RICHEY (*to* **NADIA**): Look. If you've got a mobile number or somethin' – we can get her to call you?

ELLIS: And what was it that ye needed. Are ye after some ornamental figurineens perhaps? You look the types.

FRANCIS: It's ...

ELLIS: Porcelain plates with cute kittens on?

NADIA (*cutting in*): It's the sale. The shop.

RICHEY *looks to* **ELLIS** *confused.* **ELLIS** *can't believe his ears, speaks sternly.*

ELLIS: The sale? We haven't heard of any sale. Sure – things are cheap enough as they are to be goin' slashin' the prices.

FRANCIS: The *shop*. She said the shop.

NADIA: Yes. This property. It's really quite a *brilliant* location. I *love* the –

ELLIS: I … I haven't heard tell of any of this lark. (*pause*) This hasn't been mentioned to *us*. Did *you* know about this, Rich?

NADIA: Oh, I'm sorry. We assumed you'd just be moved to another location.

ELLIS: Another location? What 'nother location?

NADIA: To volunteer?

ELLIS: I'm not a volunteer.

NADIA: Sorry?

ELLIS: I live here.

NADIA: You live here? Are you sure?

ELLIS: I definitely live here. This is me home.

NADIA: In what capacity?

ELLIS (*looking at her confused*): In what capacity? In the capacity of being living here. In that capacity. The one of being living.

NADIA: I see.

RICHEY: "Being living."

FRANCIS: Oh, we didn't know.

NADIA: We understood this to be a commercial property? Not residential?

RICHEY: That's kind of a grey area ... a point of ...

FRANCIS: Contention.

RICHEY: Yeah ...

NADIA: But wouldn't that breach some kind of ... code?

FRANCIS: It's fine. Nadia, shall we go?

NADIA: No, that *definitely* breaches the ...

FRANCIS: We'll uh, leave you to it. Come on honey, we can come back another time. (*pause*) The shop, uh, your shop looks great.

Silence.

FRANCIS (*awkwardly*): Looks great – yeah. I like what you've done with the uh ...

ELLIS: The what?

RICHEY: The space?

FRANCIS: The space. Very. Spacey.

RICHEY: Yeah – very ... (*looking to* **NADIA**) *spatial* ... innit.

Silence.

What *you* guys gonna' do wiv' it?

FRANCIS *and* **NADIA** *look then stare into each other's eyes while speaking*:

NADIA: Well, actually, we've always had this dream ...

FRANCIS: ... of starting a book-slash-record shop ...

NADIA: ... slash yoga school ...

FRANCIS: ... slash studio ...

NADIA: ... slash co-op ...

RICHEY: That's a lotta' slashes.

FRANCIS: ... with a bakery out front.

NADIA: Freshly baked pastries and ground organic coffee – from the cocoa coast of Venezuela (*they giggle*) –

FRANCIS: And a great book.

RICHEY: Right.

ELLIS: That's quite a list. Of things.

RICHEY: And what you plannin' on callin' this shop-slash-school-slash-whatever?

FRANCIS & NADIA (*pause, together*): The *Hippo Campus*.

Awkward pause.

RICHEY (*sniggers*): Er. What sorta' name is that?

NADIA (*to* **RICHEY**): It's what we're calling it.

RICHEY: That's what you're calling it? Why? That sounds gash, fam – erm ... I mean that sounds like not that er *memorable*? If I'm honest.

FRANCIS: Well, *we* think it is.

(**FRANCIS** *and* **NADIA** *turn to* **ELLIS** *and* **RICHEY** *simultaneously*)

NADIA: The hippocampus is actually the part of the brain that's used for memory. So I think it *is* quite memorable actually. Technically.

FRANCIS: We'll do book clubs, events, talks. Yoga. All sorts. Bringing the community together, you know? Co-operating.

RICHEY: A Co-op wiv' yoga?

ELLIS: Book clubs? Sure what's the point in them things?

NADIA: It's just talking about books – how they ... made you feel. About you and how you live.

RICHEY: Oh, right.

ELLIS (*beat*): Sure, books an' that – they're just a loada' oul' things said and not done, aren't they? Goin' yammerin' on about it – that's just doublin' down on the misery now, so it is. And the ... the lyin'. The "fiction".

RICHEY (*pause*): What's that got to do with anything?

ELLIS: It's exactly what we're after talking about, so it is.

RICHEY (*to* **FRANCIS**): He loves fiction really.

FRANCIS: Look, we'll come back another time, I think. It's just easier if –

ELLIS: What? Come back? When?

FRANCIS: Well, when's Sophia back? Tomorrow?

ELLIS: Tomorrow? Naw, we're closed tomorrow.

RICHEY: Are we?

(*A staring contest between* **ELLIS** *and* **FRANK** *and* **NADIA**. *A stand-off.*)

RICHEY: ... Yeah. We are.

ELLIS: Aye. Come back next week. She'll be back next week.

NADIA: Well we've got her phone number anyhows. Tha–

ELLIS: For here?

FRANCIS: Yes. (*reading*) 8-5-50-929-1?

RICHEY (*quietly*): What kinda' rhythm's that?

ELLIS (*interrupting*): No it's 9299.

NADIA: Oh.

(*pause, stand-off climaxes*)

FRANCIS: Give it a ring, wouldya babes?

NADIA *looks at phone.*

NADIA: No coverage.

FRANCIS: Here, look. What did you say it was? (*dials mobile phone*)

ELLIS: 0207 303 9299.

FRANCIS: It's ringing.

ELLIS: Me hearing's shoddy, I can't hear it. (*brief pause, too quick*) Oh, I think I hear it. Yep, that's it. All fine. It's that blasted Anastacia on the radio, so it is. Fella can't think with all that racket.

FRANCIS: I don't hear it ringing.

NADIA: No, neither do I. Is it downstairs?

ELLIS: You mean Anastacia? Will I turn it up? (*goes to move*) I will.

FRANCIS (*on phone*): Oh. Hello? (*to* **NADIA**) Someone's answered.

ELLIS (*stops*): Who? (*turns down Anastacia*)

FRANCIS: Is this – are you, is this the number – is that HOPE? (*pause, high pitched, slow*) The shop? The charity? (*longer pause, embarrassed*) Oh, um sorry about then. *I'll uh– oh,* bye now.

ELLIS: Who was that then?

FRANCIS: Wrong number. Some ... hospital. 9299 you said?

NADIA: Try the other one. The first one.

RICHEY: Nah don't. Look. I think Ellis here is a little confused.

ELLIS: I amn't confused at all.

RICHEY: The number *is* 9291.

NADIA: It is, is it?

FRANCIS: So if we call tomorrow, we can speak to Sophia about a viewing – of the rest. Yes? (*Pause*) Or would you mind at all just showing us now real quick?

ELLIS: Now I wouldn't really feel equipped to be doin' that now, y'know. I've no experience in that field. Not like your man off the telly.

FRANCIS: We can just look around? You know –

ELLIS: Y'r man Attenborough. Always in fields so he is.

FRANCIS: If that's alright? *Have a look-see.*

RICHEY: I think you mean Anna Ryder Richardson. He's always goin' on about Anna Ryder Richardson.

ELLIS: Well sure what if I am. Isn't she a talented filly for hersel' –

NADIA (*to* **FRANCIS**): I mean, it's all taken care of by the agency anyhow. (*to* **ELLIS**) This was just a courtesy, asking Sophia first. You know, common courtesy.

ELLIS: Then shall we stay courteous?

NADIA: I mean, if we could just take a look that'd be *great*. You know, if not, that's cool too, ya' know. But we've come a bit of a ways out today, from town, speaking frankly. And it *so* close to –

ELLIS: How so "town"?

NADIA: From town.

ELLIS: This *is* town.

FRANCIS: *Town*-town.

ELLIS: Now don't be bringing y'ir *town-town* talk in here.

FRANCIS: It's time off work, ya' know –

ELLIS: Ye work on Saturdays, do ye? What do ye do?

RICHEY (*cutting them off*): Right. Well, anyway. The place needs a tidy. Don' it, El. They wouldn't wannabe goin' anywhere near Hamsterdam down there now, would they, El.

NADIA: *That* sounds ominous.

FRANCIS: It's fine. We really don't mind. We'll come back.

ELLIS: No I mean, the place is a tip. (*to another customer*) That's a lovely belt. (*to* **FRANCIS** & **NADIA**) A real sty down there – that's all. (*customer hangs it up on a random rack.* **ELLIS** *picks it up, puts it aside*)

FRANCIS: We just want to see the space. The layout – in the flesh. (**FRANCIS** *moves forward toward the basement door.* **ELLIS** *moves to block.*) We pictured yoga downstairs. To start with, anyhow.

ELLIS: You *can't* go down there.

FRANCIS: Why?

RICHEY: It's private.

FRANCIS *looks to* **NADIA**. *He steps away.*

FRANCIS: Ok, look. We'll come back when Sophia's in. We don't want to cause you any hassle.

RICHEY: Looks like you already have mate.

Pause.

NADIA: Look. We'll be in touch.

RICHEY (*nicely, to* **NADIA**): Yeah I hope so. (*snidely, to* **FRANCIS**) *Her*, not you.

FRANCIS: Send our best to Sophia, please? And her little girl?

RICHEY: Yeah mate.

FRANCIS: And er – I agree. The uh "runs" – that doesn't sound like a cold. Not even close. Probably food poisoning more likely, right? Might be that barbie ya mentioned.

RICHEY: Yeah. Whatever, mate. A dodgy prawn, ay?

Shaking his head FRANCIS *exits.* NADIA *follows.*

NADIA: We'll call.

NADIA *exits, still looking around.*

RICHEY: What was that all about? Ain't needin' that right now. (*pause*) See the way she was eyein' me up, though, bruh'?

ELLIS: Wha'?

RICHEY: She wanted me mate. Could wet the sexual tension with a knife.

ELLIS: Did Sophia mention any of this to you?

RICHEY: About that *fitty*?

ELLIS: About selling the shop.

RICHEY: Nah. Musta' slipped her mind.

ELLIS: Well, obviously she *can't*. The sale. The shop. The – how ... dare she – where is it she thinks I'm to be goin' this time like. Where am I to go? Pegged back out into the street, like? With the rest of the feckin' gobshites. And with everything else going on, sure *that'd* be the worse thing.

RICHEY: Yeah, sorry mate.

A girl approaches with a blue cardigan on a hanger.

BLUE CARDIGAN GIRL (*to* **ELLIS**): Sorry, excuse me, how much is this one?

ELLIS *stares glumly down, not responding. Looks up again.*

BCG: 'Scuse me – I can't see the price of this? There's no tag.

RICHEY (*stepping in*): Priceless is it. Prob'ly 'spensive then. Hold up. (*pause*) That's er – let me see.

ELLIS *shuffles down the steps into the basement.* **RICHEY** *looks over his shoulder to* **ELLIS** *as he exits.*

BCG: Is he okay?

RICHEY (*flippant*): Just had a bit of bad news is all.

BCG: Oh, what's happened?

RICHEY: He's just been made homeless again. (*pause*) And not for the first time.

BCG: Oh, that's awful! Why?

RICHEY: Nah. He's used to it – well, he *was* used to it. He's been homeless years now. Call him Homeless Joe, they do. (*long pause*)

BCG: Homeless Joe? That sounds made up.

RICHEY (*smirking*): Yeah, nah, they don't actually call him that. Made that up. His name's Ellis. Spent a bit of time inside is all. Me mate Derek told us. All me mates know him. From prison an that.

BCG: Oh.

RICHEY: He only just got out, like not that long ago? Few weeks ago, maybe? (*becomes increasingly thrilled by taking her in with his tall tales, if only temporarily*) Like, got years inside. Used to have those teardrop tats you get, on his face? Know the ones I mean? (*pause*) Yeah. Now this news. Yeah. Hit him hard it has. Cryin' tears for real now, fam.

BCG: I see.

RICHEY: Yeah people keep sayin' that. But, no – he ain't done nothin' bad.

BCG (*hesitant*): What did he do? Do you know?

RICHEY: Killed a bloke.

BCG: Killing a guy probably *is* quite bad. What would *you* call bad?

RICHEY: Wearin' the dude's skin as a hat?

BCG: Er ...

MAN *enters carrying donations from supermarket nearby: boxes of food with reduced stickers we see later.* **MAN** *exits.*

RICHEY: Nah man, it was self-defence. If it's self-defence he don't have no choice, does he? (*to* **MAN** *leaving donations,* **MAN** *gives a nod*) Ah, sweet! Cheers bruv. Pulled pork san-widge!

BCG: How – how did he do it?

RICHEY: A bit of pipe. Pop! Dead. This guy was what they call a jocker – he was trying to er, to rape him actually. Yeah. Dude had it coming if you ask me.

BCG: Christ.

RICHEY (*starts browsing through food*): Told ya.

BCG: So why'd he still go to prison then? For manslaughter?

RICHEY (*pause, again, clearly lying*): There were some *irregularities*, apparently. (*takes bite from a sandwich*)

BCG: What irregularities.

RICHEY(*chewing*): 'Scuse me. Not eaten all day. (*pause*) Well — there weren't any witnesses.

BCG: Right. That's not that irregular. What else.

RICHEY: And um ... Old Ellis got convicted of assault, y'see — years back, though. Years back. In Ireland. In the uh, IRN.

BCG: The IR ... A? (*dubiously*) He keeps busy, doesn't he.

RICHEY: Yeah, he's a nutter mate.

BCG: He does seem a little — *unhinged*. Is he unhinged?

RICHEY: Not really no.

BCG: A little? Should he be working — I mean, does his employer know about his ... circumstances?

RICHEY: You mean his record? As'a good point actually, I don't know. Would have to get back to you on that, miss. But er — I reckon so, yeah. Although it's hard to check on an 'omeless. Not having any fixed address an' all. Guess he's kinda better off actually.

BCG (*gets out phone*): What did you say his name was again?

RICHEY: What you doin'?

BCG: Gonna' Google it. See if it got any coverage. What's the name? That's a great story, if all that's true.

RICHEY: Don't know if I should really ... You can ask him.

BCG: Oh, go on. Ellis what.

RICHEY (*pause*): Alright, alright.

BCG (*typing*): Ellis what.

RICHEY: Oh, just Ellis. Ain't got a clue.

BCG (*rolls eyes*): Ugh, really?

The **GIRL** *starts looking around on the cash desk for any evidence.*

BCG: Has he not got it written down anywhere? Where does he live?

RICHEY: What the – what are you doin', little Miss Marple?

BCG: Where does he live?

RICHEY: Here.

BCG: Here? I thought you said he was homeless. Living here. Is that allowed? Well, there must be something around then.

RICHEY: What, like fuckin' broadband bills? Nah look. You ain't gonna' find nothin' wiv' his name on.

BCG (*typing into phone*): I'll just try Ellis. Ellis. Assault. Home-less. Murder.

RICHEY: London.

BCG (*staring at phone, typing*): Lon ... don.

RICHEY (*pause, looking her up and down*): Anything?

BCG: Mmm. Don't think so. (*reading*) Wait. Here's one. Murder … a pensioner. The victim. An Alfred Wallace? Outside a soup kitchen, was it? (*shows* **RICHEY**) Is that the guy?

WOMAN *enters with bags, drops off donations. Exits.*

RICHEY: That dude's not Ellis.

BCG: No, I know that. Is that the chap he killed?

RICHEY (*squinting*): Oh. No. No don't think so.

BCG: Did you ever see the guy he killed. In a picture or something?

RICHEY: Nope.

BCG: Why are you even looking then?

RICHEY: Girl – look. Why you sticking your nose in? What's this gotta' do with you?

BCG: Just curious is all. (*puts phone behind back*) Like I said. Sounds like an interesting story – that's all, dude.

RICHEY: Well it ain't none of your business, is it. Now do you want the cardigan or not.

BCG: Or's it this one? (*reading*) Willard … Flynn? Stabbed –

RICHEY: 'Ey 'ey, I ain't discussing this no more. You takin' the cardigan or what?

BCG: Alright, alright – no need to get pissy. (*pause as* **BCG** *searches purse*) How much I owe you then?

RICHEY: For you? (*pause*) It's £1.50 for you.

BCG (*stopping with purse open*): Are you making that up? Seems a bit … cheap.

RICHEY: Fiver then.

BCG: What?

RICHEY: Fiver, I said: fiver.

BCG: Pullin' those prices outta' thin air, are ya'? Helps you bed *all* the girls, I bet. (*pause*) So just out of interest … how much is that picture over there? I like that picture. Kinda' spooky.

RICHEY: Fiver an' all. (*turning*) Yeah, fiver.

BCG: The painting?

RICHEY: (*pause*) Fiver.

BCG: Right. And that … commemorative … plate, the one with spaced-out kittens on?

RICHEY: Fivers, easy.

BCG: Everything just a fiver, is it. How about those shoes?

RICHEY (*too quickly*): Fiver. (*pause, turning*) Nah. Tenner.

BCG (*touching cardigan*): I'll give you two quid for this then.

RICHEY: Haggling? With a charity shop? That's a new low.

BCG: Well. Why not.

RICHEY: The offer stands. Fiver.

Some other customers are beginning to notice, people are leaving. The shop is quietening down.

BCG: Go on then. I'll give you the fiver. Since it's for charity. And since that fella Ellis's been made homeless again.

RICHEY (*flatly*): And not for the first time. (*politely, automatic*) Would you like a bag? They're 5p.

BCG: Can't you just chuck one in for free?

RICHEY: You're unbelievable.

BCG: I know.

RICHEY: 'Ere. (*puts fiver in old broken till – it chimes*) We got some fancy plastic bags though. So it looks like you been y'know *real* shoppin' like.

BCG *takes the cardigan, rolls it up.*

BCG: Plastic's gonna be the death of us mate. (*She turns*)

RICHEY: Thank you and you have yourself a really very nice day, miss. (*calling after her*) You know. I ain't ... (*ushering her over, quietly*)

BCG *stops and takes a precarious step backwards, clutching the cardigan.*

RICHEY: I only tell these lot I'm here on community service. But I ain't. Not really.

BCG: Oh?

RICHEY: I just ... like, like volunteering. Issa bit ... I dunno'.

BCG: It's good. Good on you. (*She rolls up the cardigan tighter*) Good for you.

RICHEY: Well.

BCG: You, um – try and find out his last name yeah? An' I'll be back. There's something there, I think. Could be something interesting there by the sounds of it.

RICHEY: Yeah, yeah – bye now.

ELLIS *peeks out as* **BCG** *exits. Pause.*

RICHEY: What you doin' peekin' there, cheeky.

ELLIS: Are they gone.

RICHEY: Is who gone?

ELLIS: That one, and the other pair.

RICHEY: Well yeah, but there's a few left. It's Saturday. That's a good thing about a Saturday.

ELLIS: No, you're right. You're right. (*pause, pointing*) Oh, what's this then?

ELLIS *comes out of the doorway and scuttles to donations.*

RICHEY: Yeah, it's cool. Why don't you come up, little feller.

ELLIS *picks out two ham sandwiches, pockets one and eats the other while searching through bags.*

ELLIS: Some daft-looking stuff that. (*pockets a few items sneakily*) Ghostbusters. They got the black fella. Look. Nice tracky suit here for you maybe, Rich. (*going through things, assessing*) Good strong belt an' all. (*pause*)

RICHEY: Oi, so what's this sale about?

ELLIS: Sure, get Sophia on the blower, would ye' now. She doesn't think we're selling up, does she? Not with all the ...

RICHEY: All the what.

ELLIS: It's comin' out of our ears so it is. Your ears. Comin' out of your ears, I mean.

RICHEY: Not my ears. What you sayin'?

ELLIS: Aye, so vicariously your ears.

RICHEY: What you on about?

ELLIS: What. (*ignoring*) Oh, look at this. This is a pretty oul' thing.

RICHEY: Look anyway – I know you ain't Irish. You think I been listening to that gash accent all this time an' believin' you?

ELLIS *looks baffled. He continues to assess the contents of the bags, starts arranging* Ghostbusters *merchandise on the window display.*

RICHEY: I couldn't give a fuck why you're putting on the Irish accent – I really couldn't – just hold it together yeah. (*laughs briefly*) This is for charity, yeah.

ELLIS *returns to the bag and pockets a couple more bits as he gets up. He holds up a dress, then finds a box. Turns from* **RICHEY** *to slowly open it.*

(**MIDDLE-AGED MAN** *passes, stops and notes what they're discussing...*)

ELLIS: Shall we put on the war video DVDs? You know. The video DVDs.

RICHEY: It's just DVD mate. And no. Don't be puttin' that bollocks on. We listenin' to strict classics na'.

ELLIS: "Cool." (*not listening, still setting up the VCR*) What'll it be then, ay' – this, maybe? (*finds a plain black box*) Oh, no. Let's look at this.

MIDDLE-AGED MAN *approaches holding a baseball cap while* **EL-LIS** *laboriously puts the DVD into the player.*

RICHEY: I just said. Don't.

MAM (*pause, looks around, whispers*): Well. Fill her up then. I'm good for it.

ELLIS (*over shoulder*): What's he after sayin'?

MAM: I, uh, I want to er …

ELLIS *plays the DVD* It's a Wonderful Life – *the anti-piracy ads and DVD menu blast into life. He struggles to turn down the volume, instead changing the channel (black & white war film), changing it again (chat show), and again* (It's a Wonderful Life)*, before giving up.*

RICHEY: *This* guy? Priest or some shit, fam. Ghostin' up like that.

MAM (*turning to* **RICHEY**, *exhausted*): This guy. This guy's had a bad week. Bad month. Bad … in*formative* years.

RICHEY: Literally ain't got a clue what you're talkin' about. Wrong number, son.

MAM: Look: I know, okay – I *know* – I'm not supposed to say anything *you know* but … *I know*, okay?

RICHEY: Know what. That you lookin' like some creepy pope-lover – or some pig, yeah. Oink.

MAM: I know ... what goes *on*. It's a perfect setup – really. Wouldn't like to see it go to waste now, would we?

RICHEY (*pause*): Funny you should say that actually mate –

ELLIS: Rich, look. (*putting his hand up to* **RICHEY**) He doesn't need to know any of that.

MAM: No. You're right. I don't. No comprendo. I just want my cap filled. 'Cos wherever I lay it – ya dig?

RICHEY: Why you talkin' like that. What's your name, sir?

MAM (*pause*): Barrett. It's Barrett.

RICHEY: Look, Barrett. (*looks him up and down*)

ELLIS: What?

MAM (*turning to* **ELLIS**): I think it'll be worth your while. Your boy knows what's what.

ELLIS: Who?

MAM: The lad.

ELLIS: You're after callin' him boy, are ye?

RICHEY: Who's he callin' boy, El?

ELLIS (*wanders over, looking down into hat as if remembering something about this man*): I think ye' should push on, mate. You've been confused.

MAM: Desire fulfilled (*getting his cash out*) a tree of life. (*pause*) How much am I peeling?

RICHEY: You really askin' for it or what, mate?

MAM *takes his hat.*

RICHEY: Yeah mate. (*to* **ELLIS**) Run him through the books.

ELLIS: What books.

RICHEY: Just yankin' yer chain. (*pause*) Anyway, boy. You look suspect. More suspect'n these creepers 'ere even. And that's a fucked-up-looking kinda' suspect. Am I right.

MAM *exits sheepishly, walking out shiftily gripping his cap, bumping into people on his way.*

RICHEY: Shit got weird, brah'. Didn't like that dude one bit. Less the likes of him's what we need.

ELLIS: Aye. And just as these pair of fecks turn up thinking they own the gaff.

RICHEY: Looks like they already do. Or will, at least. Or don't it?

ELLIS: Fine bit o' business we could do. If we don't get nicked first that is.

RICHEY: Look: Just calm down, yeah. This ain't my first rodeo, clown. *You* just need to keep your head –

ELLIS: – and not go dropping family fecking barbecues into the conversation on us, aye.

RICHEY: What?

ELLIS: Before.

RICHEY: Er – yeah. Couldn't think of anything else, could I? Y'know … It's a bit weird explaining all that like – about Edie. Puts a bit of a downer on things.

ELLIS: Would've meant a bit more sympathy though, like. Would have had them fecking off pronto instead of pestering, keepin' blabberin' on like that, you know, had you said – "No, Sophia's not here. She's in the hospital visiting a very sick friend of the family." You know.

RICHEY: Her sister.

RICHEY *gets up to serve a* **MOTHER** *with* **CHILD**.

RICHEY (*to* **MOTHER**): Would you like a bag for that?

MOTHER: Sure, yeah, please.

RICHEY: That'll be 5p.

MOTHER: Oh er … Okay. (*to* CHILD) Ellie – no, put that down.

CHILD (*holding a greeting card from a rack*): What about this one, mummy?

MOTHER: No, Ellie. You can't get nan a Cheer Up card when Grandad's died.

RICHEY: Kids, ey. (**RICHEY** *turns to* **ELLIS**) Yeah, anyway. Her sister. Not a family friend.

ELLIS: Aye, her *sister*. You remember, so? Why's not say that then – instead of family feckin' barbecues.

RICHEY (*to* **MOTHER**): Sorry about him.

CHILD: I want a funeral feckin' barbecue too, mummy!

MOTHER: Trust me, you don't. Now come on. Enough of that. It's not the weather for it, sweetie.

MOTHER *and* **CHILD** *exit.*

RICHEY: *You're* the one who said the runs. "The runs" – good one. Really good. You know. Stomach cancer or a cold. There's a bit of a divide.

ELLIS: Well I wouldn't have had t' say that now, would I – if it was anything but emergency family feckin' barbecues you were comin' out with.

RICHEY: Alright, alright. Got it. Stop saying family fucking barbecues now. Just ... please.

ELLIS: *Emergency* family feckin' barbecues. (*pause, turning*) Except she is, isn't she? Visiting poor oul' Edie. 'Cause that was the number I was after giving.

RICHEY: What? Edie? She ain't in hospital now mate. (*pause*) Wait. Does no one tell you anything? Even *I* at least know this one. (*pause*) She's at her funeral.

ELLIS: Who – Sophia? What? Sophia's funeral?

RICHEY: It's just crackin' me up for some reason. Sorry – I know I shouldn't laugh.

ELLIS *stands.*

RICHEY: I hate to be the bearer of bad news, buddy. Edie's funeral. Sophia's at Edie's funeral, mate. She put it on the calendar and e'rything. (*pause*) What. Did no one actually tell you?

ELLIS (*leaping up, goes over to calendar*): Y'what?! Hup! When?! Where?!

RICHEY (*looks at watch*): It's too late now mate. They might bring back some peng sandwiches, though. Might even be vol-au-vents.

ELLIS (*starts tearing up the calendar*): Feck!

RICHEY: What you gettin' so riled up about? Vol-au-vents are fuckin' peng, mate! Don't you know 'bout vol-au-vents?

ELLIS (*pause*) Edie. She's ...? She's (*swallows*) ... wha'?

RICHEY: No they're just stickin' her in the ground early like, savin' her the 'assle – yeah she's fuckin' dead, mate!

ELLIS *is stunned into silence. He wanders over and slumps down into his chair in front of the television, staring into the blank screen. People continue to buzz around* **ELLIS** *as he begins to weep.* **RICHEY** *helps the remaining customers.*

RICHEY: Wait. Vol-au-vents – is that one word, El?

RICHEY *continues helping customers as the TV bursts into action with the end credits of* It's a Wonderful Life.

Blackout.

Act II
Scene Two

HAVELOCK *and* EDIE's *bungalow, after her death. The interior of the room is almost identical to the shop, but the till is now an armoire, the bookshelves are laid down as a coffee table, TV table and other furniture, with a chimney stack right of stage. An archway with ornate mouldings and ledges split the room two-thirds across; the small open kitchenette off left, with windows out, and the living room, centre-right.*

HAVELOCK *is dictating a story about 'Victor and August' to himself as he approaches the house; he stands outside and recites.*

EDIE, *inside, is bundled up in a chair, face covered.*

HAVELOCK *enters house through porch door, rear right. Dim interior, blocks of orange windows fall across the wall, the only other light the television, right, on mute, aiming across centre of the room at hallway door. It beams across a shifting blue-greyish light.*

HAVELOCK, *scruffily attired, trousers with a hole in the knee, rushes in with Co-Op carrier bag in hand.*

HAVELOCK: Got some good deals, some *crackin'* deals on. (*freezes, pause, to self flatly*) Ham sangwidge ham sangwidge. (*pause*) Settle in. Be seated. Ha. (*stands a moment, side of TV*) Get the bag. Begin. (*begins to sit*). No, wait. (*stands*) Stand. Lock door, lock door. Without occasion.

A light creaking elsewhere.

Edie? That you? No. Why would it.

He walks across in front of television.

You hungry? I'm back.

He listens. He rushes across to doorway/kitchen and halts.

Just working, over here. You alright?

HAVELOCK (*to* SOPHIA, *off*): What you doing here?

SOPHIA: Getting the Complan. (SOPHIA *enters*)

HAVELOCK: Maybe in a bit. With a sangwidge.

He goes to sit. Stands. SOPHIA *moves across stage to a shelf.*

HAVELOCK *sits, goes to write at a chair, by hand, then on a typewriter, before frantically going back to a table and sketching rough portraits of* EDIE *on a pad and tearing off pages, keeping all of it in a box in front of the fireplace, beside the TV.*

He goes over to coffee table, standing, flips through notes.

(*flat*) Just working. (*touches sofa*) Why's it all wet? Ha! (*pause, sits on chair*) Don't know what's got back into me. But it's working. I'm working – Ha!

For the next minute he continues writing more, scratching head, pacing the room, mumbling. The television switches off on its sleeper timer. Light now only from streetlights.

HAVELOCK: That time already. Must be … late.

Sound of rumbling, floorboards shaking – stops. Sound of fridge door opening. A growing sense of dread.

HAVELOCK (*shout*): COMING!

He rushes off through hallway. Long pause.

HAVELOCK *comes back with large bundle of cloth, with a scalp poking out –* EDIE *–* HAVELOCK *clutching her close.*

Dry. Keep *her* dry. Keep *everything* dry.

HAVELOCK *paces, clutching, panicking slowly, before putting her by the fireplace.*

It's wet. Everywhere. (*pause*) A leak? From where? (*pause*)

A knock at the door. Silence. A knock at the letterbox. Then again, and again, growing louder.

Who – who's that? (*pause*) No. How? Of course how. Of course. Blasted nosy neighbours. Nosy. Nosy, prying … neighbours. No privacy neighbours. No …

He turns and nudges bundle of EDIE *closer to the chimney.*

The knocking ceases. Silence. The letterbox swings open and shut with the wind.

Say nothing. (*pause, shout*) Just say… (*pause*) Nothing (*pause*) – COMING!

He sweeps up EDIE *and stuffs her with great effort inside the chimney stack. The doorbell rings frantically. More knocking at the letterbox, then tapping on the glass, a silhouette briefly appears lit orange by the street-lights. Footsteps track across stones. The silhouette disappears.* HAVE-LOCK *turns to watch hallway windows. Waits.*

WHO'S IT – WHO'S THERE? LEAVE US ALONE.

Silence.

He sits in chair by coffee table, back turned to kitchen windows, and lights a candle. He begins working again.

HAVELOCK (*writing*): The *(French pronunciation) vilain (pause)* of the piece *(longer pause)* ... or is it ... *villain* ... *(pause)* vilain? *Villain?* Vil – *(pause, sigh)* word's lost all meaning.

Floorboards begin to twitch almost imperceptibly, walls creak and parts of the stage set closes in slightly with a jerk, then again, right around him.

HAVELOCK (*turning with a snap*): Low, sirs! Yes! Very low! *(pause, looking around at the set)* Well.

HAVELOCK (*starts writing faster by hand, speaking it aloud*): Bonaparte. Story's about ... the Brothers Bonaparte. *Lucien.* Joe. All the ... lads. No. The ... *brothers.* Yes. Or lovers. August, Victor ... August. *(pause)* In our august years. An Ezra Pounding. A ... McGonagall. *(pause)* Then ... Selbst ... mord.

Candle blown out.

HAVELOCK: Blast!

Relights match, it goes out.

HAVELOCK: And who're they again? Who *are* they ...

Relights match, relights candle.

HAVELOCK *twitches as if sensing someone in the room, but he doesn't look. His body closes up in fear. The sun slowly rises through windows with a deep orange light. (guttural, slow)* No ...

Candle goes out again.

HAVELOCK: No.

HAVELOCK *begins crying.*

HAVELOCK: Your august years. (*pause, through tears*) Commit. No. 'Nother word. Not ... neither. Commit. (*pause*) Commit is ... sin. Commit. *Takes.* (*longer pause*) In the hands. Life ... deferred.

Weeping, writing. Sun almost risen.

HAVELOCK: WAIT! NOT YET! (*pause*) And he began ... (*long pause*) And they ... began. (*longer pause*) And they began ... with the sun.

Sun rises, filling light into the room. He writes in silence. He fills sheets with his scribbles. Finishes, signs it. Sits and looks at the pages, pen in hand. He goes over to the archway. Measures with his hands the elevation from the floor, comparing it to his height. He removes his shoes, compares again. He's satisfied with the height. **HAVELOCK** *begins taking off his belt, stops, remembers something. He stands around. Thinking. The sun sets. He tidies the house, lining the remote up on the coffee table. He piles his pages into the box, closes it. Looks at it. Locks it. Wraps it up in gaffer tape, places it on table. Sun rises again. He stands. Sighs. Gloomily walks to the chimney. As he stands behind the TV, it flickers on, its timer kicking in again. A breakfast host talks through the morning's news. BBC news music plays.*

HAVELOCK *removes* **EDIE** *from chimney. She's covered in black soot. He coughs and splutters, places her down gently then goes back into a coughing fit. He dusts her off, places her in his chair. Voices and murmurs outside.* **HAVELOCK** *puts the box on the table before* **EDIE** *so that her head is peering downward at it.*

HAVELOCK: For ... *you.*

Doorbell rings. He freezes. Voices, off.

HAVELOCK (*sobbing*): And ... For me.

A knock at the door. Silence. Another knock. **HAVELOCK** *removes his belt, goes to move. A hard bang. Strobe flashes reveal* **EDIE**, *no longer a corpse, hanged from the ceiling right before him. Keys jangle. Voices, off. Strobes stop.* **HAVELOCK** *finishes removing his belt. By now he is sobbing.*

HAVELOCK *pulls handfuls of pills from his pockets and slams them in his mouth, chewing down on them, falling to his knees, head down, rabidly chewing.*

The door slams open. Pause. **HAVELOCK**'s *head dips, his teeth gnashing, before he suddenly passes out. The BBC News intro begins as the set closes in on* **HAVELOCK** *frozen centre stage until he is no longer visible.*

Hold spotlight on **HAVELOCK**, *now completely boxed in, singled out in the darkness.*

Blackout.

Act II
Scene Three

Lights up on a boxed **HAVELOCK** *centre stage, singled out in the spot-light. A long pause. As the lights come up, the box, similar to the one he's stored his writings and drawings in, flings open. He climbs out. He stands before the box, alone in the spotlight.*

VOICE (*off*): And what was it — that you were at?

HAVELOCK *shifts nervously, head bowed. Blackout. There's loud canned laughter.*

VOICE (*off*): When they arrived.

Lights up. The box is gone. One of the Chesterfield chairs has appeared, with its price tags. **HAVELOCK** *goes to speak, stops. Blackout.*

VOICE (*off*): Go on. (*pause*) Tell us.

Lights up. Another Chesterfield chair has appeared, price tags at-tached. Blackout.

VOICE (*off*): Speak.

Lights up. More of the charity shop set has appeared: a bookshelf, the till, etc.

HAVELOCK: I ...

Blackout.

VOICE (*off*): Go ahead. Please. Defend yourself.

Lights up. The shop is now almost complete.

HAVELOCK: I was saying (*long pause*) goodbye.

VOICE (*off*): Goodbye to …

HAVELOCK: I don't know. Who is this?

VOICE (*pause*): Oh, you're actually asking?

HAVELOCK: Well, yes.

VOICE: You're just lucky it's not you in that box. Aren't you? You should be happy. But you won't be.

HAVELOCK: That's a real boost to the self-esteem. Thanks.

VOICE: It's true, though, isn't it?

HAVELOCK: If it is, or it isn't.

EDIE (*appearing from kitchen*): Hi.

HAVELOCK: You? That was you?

EDIE: Oh, that. No.

HAVELOCK: Then who?

EDIE (*pause*): Hm.

HAVELOCK: Never mind.

EDIE: Come. Come sit with me. It's alright.

HAVELOCK: How do I know this is … not …

EDIE: I've taken something. Now. You needn't worry.

HAVELOCK: About what. What are you saying.

EDIE: I feel it working. Now I'm going to climb up, okay?

EDIE *steps tentatively onto the stool. The sound of ropes tightening.* **HAVELOCK** *goes to grab her arms, squeezes her tight and lets out a scream. Canned laughter.*

Blackout.

Act III
Scene One

Charity shop interior. Lights up, mid-argument between **RICHEY,** **ELLIS** *and* **HAVELOCK.**

ELLIS (*insistent*): No. No. You never mentioned that. You've made that bit up.

RICHEY: Fuck off I did!

ELLIS: You did!

HAVELOCK (*happily*): He didn't.

ELLIS: What? Feck off, you.

HAVELOCK: Feck *you* off. Ya' feck!

ELLIS: Her daughter's died an' all? When?

RICHEY: Fuck off, mate. You know she did –

ELLIS: ... When?

HAVELOCK *laughs, giddily excited at the news.*

RICHEY: Erm, around about the time she fell to pieces?

HAVELOCK: Remember that? Or are ye so far up your own feckin' hole you can't see for pudding?

ELLIS: Well I'll be ... So that's for why she's gone jumping front of buses?

HAVELOCK: You're a gob shite, you are. You really, really are.

RICHEY: Look't the state of her mate. Ain't been right for ages.

HAVELOCK: And I'm *certain* hasn't recovered since!

ELLIS: I thought it was because of Edie, all that. That she was all ... all weepy all'a time. I mean. Felt pretty awful about that too meself.

HAVELOCK: Unbelievable.

ELLIS: Well *you're* no better! When Edie died, ye went to feckin' pieces the worse than anny-one! Don't know what you're so feckin' giddy about.

HAVELOCK (*ignoring, pondering*): I don't know what she thinks she's at, jumping fronta' buses. But to each their own. (*pause*) And it's the last we'll see of *her* then.

ELLIS: Hope it's the last I'll see of you an all.

HAVELOCK: Right back at ye.

ELLIS (*longer pause*): The first *and* last.

HAVELOCK: That doesn't make any sense.

ELLIS: Sure it does.

HAVELOCK (*pause*): No. It doesn't.

ELLIS (*pause*): You'll see.

RICHEY: Can you two pipe down now? Fuck me. You don't even *know* what's happening with Sophia yet and you're goin' off on one, schemin'. Look, yeah. Latest things first. Not first things.

ELLIS: The mouth.

HAVELOCK: Go on then, the mouth. But I don't think there's anything you could say to dampen my high spirits today, the mouth! Oh, no!

RICHEY (*starts pacing, smiles*): Look, I knew even this wouldn't get you two shits to stop bickering like two old biddies.

HAVELOCK: He *literally* started it. With his talk.

ELLIS (*to* **HAVELOCK**): And *you*. You're worrying, you are. The sheer ... *level* ... of ... of *death* going on all around ye – and ye couldn't give *two* hoots. (*pause*) Let alone *three*, for all the dead bodies – a hoot per dead buddy, like.

HAVELOCK (*counting*): Who's three?

ELLIS: Sophia, obviously ...

HAVELOCK: Yes! Hoot! So yes! The sale *can't* go ahead!

RICHEY (*chuckles, getting a kick out of catching them out*): Nah, mate. The sale's *already done*. So if you guys've got *any* chance of makin' it now – out there – you gonna' have to do it *together*. Get me?

HAVELOCK (*shrieking*): What?

RICHEY: That happened ages ago, mate. Sorry to piss on your fireworks, mate. The sale was like ... months ago. No one tells you homelesses nothin'. You're just too fuckin' easy.

ELLIS: You *what*?!

HAVELOCK: No, she said ... (to **ELLIS**) we still had ... the day for ... to ... (*realising*) the *bitch*.

ELLIS: The *lying* bitch.

RICHEY: Whoa, whoa – calm down. She –

HAVELOCK: She knew *all* along that we were fecked. Didn't she?

RICHEY: Wait. She –

HAVELOCK: But she didn't have the balls. I'd fuckin' kill her if I could.

ELLIS: If the bitch wasn't *already* dead, like.

HAVELOCK: I'd wring the last feckin' garlicky breath of her. Outta' that *fat-arse* moonface.

ELLIS: Turfin' *us* out? We're fecking homeless, sure! How's that even happen?

HAVELOCK: And not for the first time!

ELLIS: I'm with *him* on this. The bitch.

RICHEY: Look, look. Shuddup a minute.

HAVELOCK: I'm seething so I am.

ELLIS: And so am I!

They make seething noises together.

RICHEY: ... Rrright. So first of all, she *ain't* dead – you fucked-up idiots are *mental*. (*pause*) I only said that shit about 462s because you're a pair of fucking dickheads which you've just gone an' proved to me. So thanks, in a way. But latest things first now (*pause*) you're fucked, the pair of you. *And* you deserve it. And if I'm honest, that makes it absolutely fine. I'm cool with this. This is the end at least, innit.

Long pause.

HAVELOCK (*hollow, distant, shaking head*): What? I ... I ... it can't be.

RICHEY: Oh, belee' me.

HAVELOCK: That's it. That's it. (*pause*) I'll not go back to that. I'll not go back out there. No fucking way.

ELLIS: I hope *she* fuckin' dies first. All dramatic on the whajacallit operating table, like. To give her a glimmer of hope first, ya' know like – but then like a lost spinal cord or something. 'Cause that's bang outta' order that is.

RICHEY: Do you not get it? She ain't been hit by a bus, you twat. (*pause*) She's at a family barbecue actually. Proper wash out, though, I'll bet.

ELLIS: Eh?

RICHEY: Happy fuckin' new year, cunts. Have a good one. (*pause*) Weird sayin' that a week late. But everything's a week late for you pair'a twats.

HAVELOCK: She's not coming to say goodbye, is she.

RICHEY: No mate. She said it was hard enough sayin' goodbye to this place. Because you two dickheads're still in it.

ELLIS: She said that, did she? That's rich, the dickhead bitch. (*pause*) And what kinda plan would that have been then, gettin' us to stop quarrelling – when we found out she wasn't dead at all? Ya feckin' eej. Didn't think *that* one through.

RICHEY: I kinda' hope you rot, you know. I kinda' hope that. Later. (*goes to leave.*)

ELLIS: What the fuck do I care if a drug-dealing scally wants me to rot? So don't think you're getting off that lightly. The things I have on *you*, boyo.

RICHEY (*turning*): What if I just fuckin' knock you out now, cunt?

ELLIS: Go on then. Hit me, ye feck. On community service. Where'd that end ya up? (*pause*) Ya' black feck!

(*long pause*)

RICHEY: Look, I'm off. I *actually* came here to tell you you coulda' stayed at my bro's place for the time bein'. He's moving to Luxembourg (*pause*). He likes it there the weirdo. But *fuck that*. I can't stand you two fucking pricks. You *deserve* each other.

RICHEY *exits.*

RICHEY (*shouting, off*): Don't forget to lock the shutters, bitches!

Door slams.

ELLIS: Good riddance. (*pause*) The feck! Oh, I'll fix him. Just a quick visit from the guards'll sort *that* out.

HAVELOCK (*pause*): For the record, I'd never have done anything ever to deserve you. Not even if – if I was on BBC radio and touching little 'uns on the regular.

ELLIS: They can feck off the both of them. The dickhead bitches, the pair. (*pause*) I always said we should have killed her, y'know. So now I'm glad we didn't, because a fat lot of difference that woulda made. And the mess to deal with as well, on top of all this. That'd only be making things worse, sure.

HAVELOCK: Where are we going to go? What are we …

ELLIS: We? There is no 'we'. Oh no, sonny. There's no 'we' in team.

HAVELOCK: What? (*pause*) But ... there's a 'mate'. In team.

ELLIS: There is no 'we' – or *mates* – annymore. You're a leeching gobshite so you are – and I want nothing more to do with ye.

HAVELOCK: Your mouth really is a horrid, dead place, El.

ELLIS (*beat*): Like your wife's fanny.

HAVELOCK: What?

ELLIS: I was just after saying ...

HAVELOCK (*searching on floor*): I know what you said! (*pause, visibly hurt*) You've really taken it too far this time. Too far by one step. A big step!

ELLIS: And a *nice* dead horrid place it was too. Your wife's fanny I'm still referring to.

HAVELOCK (*finds picnic knife*): Shut your mouth. Now.

ELLIS: She wanted H, yeah? Tick it off her list? Yeah – but that was just the H what starts with *Heroin*. You know what else she wanted to do before she died? You know what else was on that list?

HAVELOCK: No.

ELLIS: She made me *swear* never to tell you. Aye.

HAVELOCK: Who the –

ELLIS: Right here as well. While she was 'volunteering'.

HAVELOCK: She'd ... no. Stop.

ELLIS: Up against the till. Coppers jangling about. (*pause*) Her tits jangling about. *Volunteered* her services, so she did. (*pause*) And you do remember that 'E' on her list?

HAVELOCK: There *was* an 'E' on her list.

ELLIS: Yep.

HAVELOCK: I thought that was Ecstasy.

ELLIS: She had that an all. You were there.

HAVELOCK: She did, yes. She took that. I watched her. Had a grand oul time. Calmed her right down it did. Kept licking me cheeks like a helpless little white-hair kitten, pawing away at me.

ELLIS: Yeah. You're right. She *did* take that. (*winking, pointing at his crotch*) But you didn't get to watch *that* one. You just helped her die. I let her *live*.

(*long, murderous pause as if something has been forever broken*)

HAVELOCK: Go. Fetch the box. (*from his inside jacket pocket, he tosses* ELLIS *the key*)

ELLIS (*confused*): What? Really? Ye mean now?

HAVELOCK: Now. Get it.

ELLIS (*pause, cautious*): Aye. Aye. I'll give ye a little time to cool yir jets, will I? I will. Before we go ahead and do anything drastic. Maybe too far it was taken this time. By one step. Just a little one.

ELLIS *edges away cautiously, exits downstairs rear.*

HAVELOCK *removes his suit jacket. Tosses it on the chair, the price tag visible.*

HAVELOCK (*smiles dimly*): The quiet. (*pause*) The quiet's all I ever needed. The privacy.

He unbuckles his belt.

HAVELOCK (*pause*): I never understood … Why they fold everything up. For the poor soul who finds it? Or's it just one small dignity, torn from a life of none.

He pulls out the belt. He peers down as if expecting the trousers to fall. But they remain sat loosely about his waist, still quite snug.

HAVELOCK (*looking down*): The shoes – a vital few inches.

He kicks off his shoes as if after a long day at work. They disappear behind a shelf.

HAVELOCK: And the socks. For luck.

He removes his socks and tosses them aside. **HAVELOCK** *ties a tight knot with the belt around the handle of the shutter which has been left 3/4s up. The belt's price tag dangles about his mouth.*

HAVELOCK: What can you give a man who has nothing at all in this world?

Pause.

HAVELOCK: What can you give a man who's nothing in this world, I ask.

He reaches his long arms to the shutters' button. He can't quite reach. He struggles for a few moments, taking an almost comical run up with the belt around his neck, clawing at the controls, still not reaching, but almost there.

Best o' luck with the new place then.

He finally reaches with one final stretch. During the ensuing moments, HAVELOCK *presses and holds the shutters so they rise up slowly, lifting his feet. His trousers slowly open about his waist but do not fall. This is shortly before he smashes the shutter's button with a fist, and up they snap, choking him between the door and the shutters.*

ELLIS (*off, laboriously coming up the stairs*): Here it is! Still unopened. Just as ye left it. It'll be great craic openin' her'up, so it will. Finally. We'll have to call that dickhead-bitch Richey back to see it too. (*pause*) Doubt he'll come, mind. The lazy poof. What you reckon? Hal? C'mon, Hal! I didn't mean that about Edie. I was only ... She'd never –

ELLIS *enters to see a hanged* HAVELOCK. *Only sound is the whirring shutters. As* ELLIS *covers his mouth, a strobe flash as the whirring grows louder. The shutters fizzle, spark, then fall silent. The television blinks on: BBC News. At the sound of the theme tune,* ELLIS *turns, shrieks and sprints towards the door still clutching the case. He realises it's just the television and calms down a little, but he's still spooked. As* ELLIS *approaches the door, he takes a long look at* HAVELOCK, *before crawling between* HAVELOCK's *dangling legs to flee the scene.* HAVELOCK *chokes out, legs kicking a little, until one last stretch of the leg stiffens him up. The sun dims behind him.*

Fade to black, only the television in the darkness:

TV NEWS READER (*off*): An elderly man found hanged in a high-street charity shop has been identified as local volunteer Dr Henry Havelock, according to police coroners.

Betting shop manager Oliver Schreiner made the discovery when he noticed feet dangling from the high-street storefront early on Tuesday afternoon.

RAY: I was 'aving a fag an' I seen 'im ... 'anging there. They're usually closed bank holidees, y'see, but not us. (*cough*) By the time I get over there to take a peek, y'know there's nothin' I could do for him. At all. Y'know he'd gone all blue an' stiff an' that. We rung the ambulance and they come pick him up. (*pause*) Pretty harrowin' business, all that.

INTERVIEWER: Did you know Dr. Havelock personally?

RAY: Didn't know he was no doctor, no. Well I seen him 'anging about that shop most days yeah – sorry, no pun intended. (*pause*) I give him a Fanta once, pink one. Seemed a gentle sorta type, y'know, bit confused maybe. Nice enough for an 'omeless."

TV blacks out.

Act III
Scene Two

Bookshop/café/yoga school interior: The Hippo Campus. The H is the same as the former HOPE *sign.* NADIA *serves stage-right at the counter where a* CUSTOMER *is buying a pasty, deciding what crisps to have, umming and ahhing over Cheese & Onion or Salt & Vinegar.* FRANCIS *busies himself wiping tables, then writes the specials board in chalk, with a reminder about the first yoga/book club for* Eat Pray Love *along the bottom, and a demented-looking smiley face.*

The café atmosphere is off-key. Washed out, dreamy music plays. The actual smell of coffee is in the air. Another customer sits at a table, sipping a latte and poking at a sandwich.

Centre stage, a twee little table sits between two red Chesterfield chairs, among an array of calculatedly random, upcycled furniture within the café interior. All the furniture, light fittings and decor are for sale, with price tags hanging from all angles. The bookshelves have been replaced with shiny new ones, stacked with books on yoga, mindfulness, meditation and a Top 10 'We recommend ...' section with books about Israel-Palestine by Noam Chomsky, John Pilger and Robert Fisk.

NADIA: Now are you sure you don't want that meal deal? You can pick any drink for just 20p. We call it the "Chompsky".

CUSTOMER: Nah, you're alright. Just the pasty and crisps, ta.

NADIA: Or perhaps something to read? (*pointing*) Boris Johnson's tell-all is pretty hot right now. He'll do anything for a few quid, let's face it.

CUSTOMER: Yeah, nah. Not a fan. (*reaching for the pasty*) I'm just gonna ...

NADIA: Or. How about something more ... agreeable. Michael Palin?

CUSTOMER: Nah, you're alright, ta.

She hands over the pasty and crisps.

CUSTOMER: Bye then.

NADIA (*over-eager, too loud*): Have a lovely day!

Anastacia – "Left Outside Alone" begins to play. Swaying gently at first, **FRANCIS** *and* **NADIA** *begin to nod and mime exaggeratedly in unison, before laughing together, then going back to staring hollow-eyed in their places and returning to wiping tables and doing busy work as* **BLUE CARDIGAN GIRL** *enters (now wearing blue cardigan). The doorbell wind-chime sounds.*

FRANCIS *works towards the door, wiping tables with a dirty dish cloth.* **BLUE CARDIGAN GIRL** *goes up to the counter and picks out a cake, sits and eats. A handful of people come in, look about curiously, before strolling out again; the café finding that slow, lurching rhythm of an ailing new business while the cheesy muzak continues.*

Wearing all black, a **SHROUDED MAN** *with* **HAVELOCK**'s *chest tucked under his arm staggers through the door, head dipped, as if still in procession from a funeral. He lowers into one of the Chesterfields. Spotting the price tag on his jacket sleeve, he pulls it off and tosses it onto the little table. He stares blankly a moment, stands up. He moves with purpose toward the counter and starts grabbing at vol-au-vents laid out on a platter, gorging himself.*

FRANCIS: *Mate?* Hey *mate?* (*going over*) You can't just stand there, hey mate, gorging yourself without payin', *mate.* This ain't a non-prof, dude. (*grabs his arm*) You gotta *pay* for those.

Turning with a snap, the **SHROUDED MAN** *puts the box down on the right-hand Chesterfield, and removes his hood, hat, second hat, another hat, and scarf, then another scarf. Beneath is* **ELLIS. BLUE CARDIGAN GIRL** *begins to take notice, watching the altercation.* **ELLIS** *is just about done taking off all his gear when a* **CUSTOMER** *sweeps in the front door, the sound of a whipping gale running up behind her. The door closes. The music stops. Now in the silence:*

ELLIS (*with a cockney accent*): You're alright fella. We're with the funeral lot.

FRANCIS *doesn't have a response and stutters as* **ELLIS** *moves across to the Chesterfield and sits back down. He fiddles with the box nervously as he looks around, still chewing.*

BLUE CARDIGAN GIRL *downs the rest of her coffee, stands and moves quickly over to* **ELLIS**. *He busies himself with putting the scarves and hats back on.*

BCG: Excuse me. You're that man. The volunteer here, right? (*pause*) Who was unwell (*catching herself*) ... or something. Right?

ELLIS (*distractedly*): Wha'?

BCG: That ... young guy, who used to be here, tall dude, when it was a charity shop. He said. D'you remember? He told me about you. How are you? You keeping okay?

ELLIS (*back to his cod-Irish accent*): I'm grand, sure. Do I not look grand, so?

BCG: You do, you do. You look fine. (*quietly*) In an ... unhinged sort of way.

ELLIS: Unminged is it?

BCG (*quickly*): What's that, in your box?

ELLIS: This? Me box? This is nothin'. Just a ... memento [*pronounced:* mimento]. I was after goin' openin' it actually, before ye so rudely interrupted.

BCG: I'll give you a fiver for it. Whatever it is.

ELLIS: Sure it's not for sale is it, little girl?

BCG: Nah'm just kidding! That was meant as a joke. That's what the other guy used to say. "Everythin' for a fiver." Kind of a weird ... in-joke. Don't know why I thought you'd get that.

BCG *perches in the opposing chair and watches. She's more interested in the man than the box.*

ELLIS: I'd hazard there isn't much "to get" by the sounds of things.

BCG: I wanted to ask, actually. If you don't mind.

ELLIS *is only half-listening. He's unpeeling the tape from around the box and pulling it open.*

BCG: Would you be interested in doing an interview, with me that is? For a magazine. We're doing a series. On the homeless. Elderly homeless specifically.

Frustrated by the box, ELLIS *begins to lash out.*

ELLIS: Sure amn't I both of those things. You needn't go tellin' me all about elderly and homelesses!

ELLIS *finally pulls the box open. Paper falls out onto the table, across the floor.*

ELLIS: Sure amn't I the very last person that'd be news ta?

BCG: Oh no no. Sorry. I think you've misunderstood. It's ... um. (*pause*) What're you looking for there?

ELLIS *sifts greedily through the papers, as if searching for something of value – anything but notepaper. He scatters much of it on the table in his haste.* BCG *picks up a sheet and reads out loud.*

BCG: "The Well of Loneliness" (*scanning the text, she flicks through another, pauses*) ... "Hallelujah Hand-me-down" ... Did you write these? Prose pieces are they? Or essays, maybe.

ELLIS: Em ...

BCG (*still scanning the manuscript*): This is really ... Edie's your wife?

ELLIS: Em?

BCG: ... Fascinating. Are they all different? *And* illustrated?

ELLIS: The ... Wha'? Yeah. (*lying*) Yeah all different.

BCG: That's ... mad.

ELLIS: Mind who y're callin' mad, missy.

BCG: Hold on. Just a mo. Lemme make a call, two ticks.

BCG *nips outside frantically thumbing at the screen of her phone.*

ELLIS *sees an envelope amongst it all, and removes the letter.*

BCG (*off, putting phone to her ear*): Hey. It's me.

ELLIS *begins to read silently to himself. Spotlight on* ELLIS *as he reads.*

HAVELOCK'*s voice reads the letter:*

HAVELOCK (*off*): Dearest Ellis,

If you're reading this (*pause*) well. You know what I've done. So, I shall keep this short, as I know you do not read well. Nor do you enjoy reading particularly. (pause) Likely because you are so poor at it.

ELLIS (*shouting at the letter in his hand*): Feck off, you!

HAVELOCK (*off*): These papers, this writing, of mine. Here. That you hold in your hand. I bequeath to you. Bequeath means give but never mind that for now. (*pause, sigh*) This final piece is the culmination of my life ... and my wife's ... work. This. Is our ... magnum opus. (*pause*) *Opi. Opises. Magnum opises.*

ELLIS: What sorta ice cream's that then?

HAVELOCK (*pause*): ... Masterpiece. And I knew that you, being you, would devise to pilfer it and claim it as your own. (*Pause.*)

ELLIS (*pause*): *Me? Pilger it?!*

HAVELOCK (*off*): So this letter ... is how I win. Dictated not read. Dr Henry Havelock.

ELLIS (*pause, desperately, then realising*): Well! Ain't pilgered nothin', have I Doctor what-a-cock? When it was you goin' pilgerin' me feckin' home, ya feck!

ELLIS *pulls the matches from his pocket, struggles at first to light one, then strikes up a few at once.*

ELLIS: Now we'll see who's pilgerin' what.

FRANCIS *moves forward as* ELLIS *sets the papers alight, holding them high as they burn.*

FRANCIS (*shrieking*): The fuck, mate?

The smoke alarm sounds. FRANCIS *yelps with the rag in his hand.* BCG, *seeing the flames, comes bursting back into the café, speechless, hand-over-mouth in front of the little fire.* ELLIS *throws the burnt sheets down. The wind picks up and the place starts to go up quickly, the sound of the licking flames more so than visible fire.*

BCG: You made copies, right?

ELLIS (*pause*): Do I look the type who's makin' copies, eh?

NADIA *storms over with the fire extinguisher and blasts it in* ELLIS's *direction, hitting him in the face, along with the box, his hands, and the chair, covering it all white with foam.* ELLIS *yelps. Long pause before* ELLIS *starts to laugh and laugh ... and laugh.*

Long pause while ELLIS *shifts from cackle to chuckle.*

BCG (*ignoring the laughter, exiting*): Well, there's plenty more where that came from. (*to no one in particular*) That homeless 77-year-old poet philosopher in Brazil, for one. (*pause, pulls open the door*) Laters.

Door slams. Bells chime.

FRANCIS (*to* ELLIS): The fuckin' hell's wrong with you, mate? Funeral or no funeral – you're gettin' the fuck offa my property! (*pause, he doesn't move*) Go on! Rack off, old man!

FRANCIS *forces* ELLIS, *still covered in foam, out the door with much to-do.*

The door slams again, sounding the bells a final time. Then silence. FRANCIS *sighs, wiping the residual foam off his clothes and hands.*

FRANCIS: Looka the state of this place.

Anastacia – "I'm Outta Love" drops in.

FRANCIS: Really? Anastacia? Again??

NADIA: Come on. *(dancing as Richey and Ellis did in the shop)* You know you love it.

The volume cranks up. **NADIA** *is miming and swaying.*

FRANCIS *(finally joining in)*: Ah fuck it. This shit is my *jam*!

The music continues. Blackout.

Act III
Scene Three

Empty floor. No shop, no café. A bundled corpse centre stage, under a harsh spotlight. A pause of around 30 seconds. The corpse stirs, wriggles a little here and there. The sound of heavy breathing grows. Eventually, and with much effort, the corpse climbs to its feet and slowly unbundles itself.

HAVELOCK (*as he emerges coyly*):

There was a Poet whose untimely tomb
No human hands with pious reverence reared,
But the charmed eddies of autumnal winds
Built o'er his mouldering bones a pyramid
Of mouldering leaves in the waste wilderness —
A lovely youth — no mourning maiden decked
With weeping flowers, or votive cypress wreath,
The lone couch of his everlasting sleep —
Gentle, and brave, and generous — no lorn bard
Breathed o'er his dark fate one melodious sigh:
He lived, he died, he sung, in solitude.
Strangers have wept to hear his passionate notes,
And virgins, as unknown he passed, have pined
And wasted for fond love of his wild eyes.
The fire of those soft orbs has ceased to burn,
And Silence, too enamoured of that voice,
Locks its mute music in her rugged cell.

Blackout.

End.

ACKNOWLEDGEMENTS

DT: Thank you to the good people at Muswell Hill Soup Kitchen and Oxfam Victoria, Charlie at Montag Press, Mark Marquardt (Akte One), Michael and Sarah, David L. Williams, Jilna, Björn at planpolitik, Sanjay, Josiah Flynt Willard, Diana Marossek of Street Art Berlin, my P & M – and of course, as of July 2017, my wonderful, intrepid, comic genius of a wife, Vera. I hope it made you chuckle darkly.

ELLIS: Ahem. And are ye not forgetting annyone?

DT: Oh, sorry – deep gratitude goes to the bizarre, mischievous mind of Dr. Havelock Ellis. Obviously.

ELLIS: Aye. A right mentalist so he was.

DT (*long pause*): Aye.

About the Author

Declan Tan is a writer, editor and journalist based in Berlin. His work has appeared in *Little White Lies*, *Huck* magazine, *The Daily Telegraph*, *Flaunt*, and others. This is his first play.